The Recollections of Sir James Bacon:
Judge and Vice Chancellor, 1798-1895

Edited by
Juliette de Marcellus

The Recollections of Sir James Bacon: Judge and Vice Chancellor, 1798-1895

Edited by
Juliette de Marcellus

Academica Press
Washington~London

.

Library of Congress Cataloging-in-Publication Data

Names: de Marcellus, Juliette (editor) | Bacon, James (author)
Title: The recollections of sir james bacon : judge and vice chancellor,
1798-1895 | Juliette de Marcellus (editor), Bacon, James (author)
Description: Washington : Academica Press, 2024.
Identifiers: LCCN 2023949547 | ISBN 9781680535327 (hardcover) |
9781680535341 (paperback) | 9781680535334 (e-book)

Foreword

Sir James Bacon (11 February 1798 – 1 June 1895) was a British judge and Vice Chancellor of the Court of Chancery. Bacon was born at Somers Town, London. His father had gone there from Holt, Norfolk, to work as an attorney's clerk in Clerkenwell. Bacon received part of his early education in Holt. He left school at twelve and worked for some years in the same attorney's firm, Rhodes and Cook.

On 4 April 1822, Bacon joined Gray's Inn and was called to the bar on 16 May 1827. As an impecunious young barrister, he engaged in much literary work, including the first English translation of Victor Hugo, as well as a pseudonymous *Memoires of the Life and Writings of Lord Byron*, which breached copyright. The publisher, John Murray, decided not to sue because copyrighted works of doubtful moral character had become precarious following the case of William Lawrence. This work was illustrated by George Cruikshank, whom Bacon knew, one among the many literary and artistic personalities in his circles of friends and acquaintances, which included Charles Lamb and Mary Shelley. Bacon also wrote as a journalist for the *Times of London*.

Bacon switched to Lincoln's Inn in 1833 and became a bencher on 2 November 1846, soon after "taking silk" and becoming a Queen's Counsel (QC). In 1859, he became undersecretary and secretary of causes to the Master of the Rolls. Bacon became the Chief Judge for Bankruptcy under the Bankruptcy Act of 1869 and held this post until the act was repealed and jurisdiction over bankruptcy was transferred to the Queen's Bench Division.

Bacon became Vice Chancellor in 1870. The following year, he was knighted and appointed to the Privy Council. The post of Vice Chancellor was abolished by the Court of Judicature Act of 1875, but he retained the title until he retired in 1886, at the age of 88. He died on 1 June 1895, at the age of 97. During his career, Bacon was celebrated for his caustic wit. One curt example came when a decision of his was

The Recollections of Sir James Bacon:
Judge and Vice Chancellor, 1798-1895

appealed. The only item in his notes to the higher court was a cartoon of the appellant and the words, "This man is a liar."

Bacon married Laura Cook, daughter of the attorney for whom both he and his father worked as clerks, in 1827. She died in 1859. For many years they were at home at Compton Beauchamp House in what is now Oxfordshire. The couple had four sons, two of whom predeceased the judge, and one daughter. Bacon's descendants included his granddaughter, Susan Lawrence, one of the first woman Labour Party MPs, and A. A. Gordon Clark, a county court judge and celebrated author of detective novels and short stories under the pseudonym, Cyril Hare.

Sir James's *Recollections* have been transcribed from his unpublished memoirs, typed by his granddaughter, Lydia Bedford (*née* Lawrence), on an early model typewriter. I wish to thank the technical staff at the Society of the Four Arts in Palm Beach, Florida, for their help in this endeavor.

Juliette de Marcellus, Palm Beach, September 2023

THE RECOLLECTIONS
OF SIR JAMES BACON

Say what you will! — Growing old brings with it many disagreeable reflections and many regrets. I would not, however, be thought so unreasonable, or so unthankful, as to forget or deny that this, the inevitable lot of humanity, is not *all* disagreeable, or *all* the subject of bitter regret. On the contrary, I am truly sensible of the many causes of thankfulness which fill my heart—lend solace to my griefs, and help me to bear the burthens which failure of strength—the subsidence of animal spirits –the vanishing of all earthly hopes and earthly happiness cast upon my weakened frame.

Nor need I say, in this place, that in pouring forth my regrets for what I have lost I do not forego the blessed hope that, in another world, all that seems strange, or imperfect in this, will fade into nothingness and will be replaced by such glories and joy and happiness as no mortal soul can conceive – no mortal tongue can tell.

December 1886

Looking away from generals to particulars, I am led, at this moment, to consider some of the former events of my life – I do so with great misgivings; and, but for the persuasion I am under, that my present scribbling will not meet other than affectionate and indulgent eyes, I should not venture to occupy (I can hardly way waste) my time in my present employment.

Retrospection is not always satisfactory. The effect of time must necessarily be to dim the memory, – all the things which formerly presented themselves have lost their dur proportion with the fading of the objects – their true colours have faded and woefully changed – the warm medium through which they were regarded has become cooled – and sometimes their ashes have ceased to retain any of their wonted heat. Besides these inevitable changes, the ever active fancy, without meaning to play falsely, will interpose its illusions, and cannot be trusted to narrate faithfully things as they really were. Autobiographies are seldom truthful – not because the vanity of their authors betrays them into willful misrepresentation – but because the memory's soft features fade away before the brighter lights of imagination.

Under the full conviction of the truth of these principles I will try to tell as well and as truly as I can some of the passages of my long existence.

Childhood

My earliest recollection is of a small house in Weston Place, St. Pancras, in the road leading from Battle Bridge (now called King's Cross) towards the old St. Pancras Church – and directly opposite to the Small Pox Hospital. The family consisted then of my father and mother, and one sister, Betty, older by eight years than any of the other children, and of one brother (Henry). My mother's mother formed a part, and a very important part of the family, by whom then, and for several subsequent years, the cares of looking after and the bringing up of the children were most admirably discharged. She was a person of stature above the middle size – powerful and clever in all things – of venerable aspect, great good temper and beloved by all around her. By birth a Lancashire woman, she retained her country habits and her native dialect. Many of her most valuable precepts and proverbs remain firmly fixed in my memory, and have not unfrequently reminded me of most valuable principles by which human conduct ought to be regulated.

My father, who was a skillful and able conveyancer, was engaged in a department of a celebrated attorney's establishment – and was of necessity absent during the greater part of the day. My mother conducted a somewhat extensive business as an embroiderer of muslin – a business which has long ceased to exist having been superseded by the perfection of mechanical contrivances which have taken the place of the deft and laborious needle by which wondrous exploits were then performed. From the profits made by the united industry and skill of my parents, they were enabled to bring up their family – rapidly increasing – in perfect comfort and content – though far enough from any approach to affluence. To make both ends of the year meet were all they could hope for and probably all that they desired.

Of the persons who may have frequented the house, I have no distinct recollection except a certain portly old gentleman called Dr. Wachsell, a German, but an English physician – the principal officer and resident in the neighboring hospital which had been establish for the purpose of diffusing publicly the benefits of the then somewhat novel practice of vaccination. All that I know or can remember of him is that he was very kind and that his visits were most agreeable to everybody in the house.

It must have been quite early in this 19th century (I cannot fix a more certain date) that we changed our abode to The Polygon in Somers Town – a plot of houses then newly built, one of which – No. 10, with a somewhat spacious garden behind – we inhabited – and where we lived very happily for about ten years. Somers Town was then a mere suburb – bounded on the south by what was called the New Road (extending from Paddington to Battle Bridge) on the North by wide open fields, occupied by a famous Dairy Farmer named Rhodes – and extending to what was and is called Camden Town. The Hampstead Road, a mere extension of Tottenham Court Road, was the Western boundary and the left consisted of the road to Highgate through Kentish Town. At the time I am now referring to, Somers Town was in some degree a sort of French Colony. The great Revolution had brought to it a great many French emigrants of various degrees – noblemen, ladies, artisans – found there a refuge, and the more able and industrious of them found the means of existence; the others depended upon a scanty subscription by the British government. A ladies boarding school was established under the care of a marquise whose name I forget but whose reputation stood very high among her compatriots, and whose charitable exertions were highly prized by the poorer inhabitants of the district. A chapel (Roman Catholic) was built and the spiritual wants of the community were admirably conducted by a certain portly ecclesiastic of great piety – and admirable presence – and whatever his real rank and name may have been as the Abbé Caron. I do not remember any further particulars about this colony – I have a very clear recollection that it was held in great respect and esteem by the Protestant inhabitants, which I am led to believe could only have been acquired by the good conduct of these exiles.

One of the inhabitants of the Polygon was of sufficient notoriety to make his name remarkable even among the little people there. William Godwin was at that time spoken of as a marked personage. The horrors of the French Revolution were talked of in a manner which made us children wonder and sometimes shudder, – and with these things the name of Godwin was always associated. The slaughter of the poor French King – and the seditious proclivities of no inconsiderable portion of the English – were all supposed to be represented in the persons of Godwin and his wife – the famous Mary Wollstonecraft – and nothing was contemplated in the nursery more diabolic than these Demos who had become our neighbours. Our fears were somewhat quieted by the sudden death of the poor woman who died in childbirth of that ill-fated daughter who subsequently became the wife of Percy Bysshe Shelley. In rambling over the crowded burying-ground of old Pancras Churchyard we could not repress a feeling of terror at passing by the grave of Mary Wollstonecraft. The Churchyard was a frequent walk and the spelling out the name of the illustrious dead an occupation of some interest. The somewhat ostentatious monument of Pascal di Paoli – the Corsican patriot excited our admiration and the epitaph chiseled upon the tombstone of a departed attorney failed to give us a very exalted opinion of the work of that profession, which it was my future fate to be closely connected with. His name I forget – but the "the piece of elegy and fame" were supplied by this verse.

> Here lies on – believe it if you can –
> Who, though a lawyer, was an honest man.
> To him the gates of Heaven 'ere open'd wide,
> But shut to all his tribe beside.

It is in vain to try to recollect what happened during the years of our residence in this place. All that I do remember is that they must have been very pleasant – that all or path was peace. Many children were there born – the more it seemed the merrier. Joys abounded – but they were all circumscribed within our own circle. Friends or acquaintances we had very few. Amusements beyond Christmas – Twelfth Night – The Pantomime at Sadler's Wells, have left very slight impression on my mind – and of sorrow or care we knew nothing.

I must have learned to read from my grandmother; I cannot recollect the process by which this was accomplished, but I do know that I was able to read to her in the only book I ever saw her use. In my mind's eye I see it now! A good-sized octavo, in large print – Thomas à Kempis in English with an engraving of the crucifixion after Van Dyke. The only other book I remember at this early period was a sturdy quarto in black leather *The Faerie Queene* with wood cuts. I must have read this since reading was one of my very earliest occupations, and I remember the Knight and the Dragon – but it would be untrue to say that at that time I had any notion of the "gentle knight pricking on the plain" beyond what the uncouth cuts conveyed to my eye. However, I did (Heaven knows how) master the black-letter text, and for aught I know to the contrary, Dogberry was right in asserting that "reading and writing come by nature."

How, – by what steps – and in what manner knowledge of all kinds finds its way into the human mind is a mysterious affair – all we can say about it is that such as we have been able to acquire is there; and while we thank God for such of it as falls to our share we ought to pray that we may be able to make its employment as useful and profitable as may be.

The first experience I had of the world beyond the very limited sphere of the Polygon, consisted of a journey to the town of Holt, in Norfolk – my father's native place. An old friend of his was Mark Massingham, who carried on there the humble trade of a baker and corn dealer. He was quite an old man and lived with his two spinster daughters, old maids. One of them, having paid a visit at our house, proposed to take me back with her – and it would be a good thing for me – her offer was accepted. I therefore accompanied her to Holt and remained for a year or thereabouts under her care; and very kind and gentle care it was. Here for the first time I began to appreciate the beauties of the country. I have no reason to think that the neighbourhood was in any remarkable degree picturesque, but it was perfectly rural – a wide open common – a small wood full of wild flowers – primroses, cowslips, bluebells and all the other children of the spring were for the first time introduced to my acquaintance and a good deal of time was most pleasantly spent in wandering about the fields with unrestrained delight.

Nor was it merely in idleness that my whole time was spent. Holt was endowed with a Free Grammar School (one of Edward VI's as I have since learned) and of this I became a pupil and here was I first introduced to the Eton Latin Grammar of which I was taught to learn some part of the accidence, while reading the Bible and repeating the Catechism formed a part of the daily exercise. The boy in the school – all children of the Townspeople numbered about 30 – and by them I was initiated into the delights of marbles and leapfrog and trap-ball, but I do not recollect that cricket had at that time been established among our sports. But that of which I retained the liveliest recollection was the delightful ride which I frequently had in surrounding villages. The course lay over salt marshes extending to the sea – wide and wild – of the very wet – commanding views of the low-lying shore and displaying the white cliffs of Cromer in the extreme distance, treeless and flat with no remarkable feature except the old and time-worn remains of the ghastly gibbet on which a notorious malefactor had been executed about a century before. In the sunshine this sight was striking – but in the face of a keen East win – with a dark sky and a driving sleet, the appearance of "Salter's Gibbet" made an impression on me which I could almost shudder at the recollection of, even now.

School Days

This experience must have taken place when I was between five and six years old, and I suppose I must have attained the latter age when my dear good old maid brought me back in the stagecoach – a long day's journey – and restored me to my dear mother in the Polygon.

It was then determined that my serious education should be fun and, a boarding school having been recommended to my father, I was transferred to Gordon House, Kentish Town, kept by a Scotchman, one Andrew Mensall. I don't think that schoolmasters in general leave very agreeable memories in the minds of their pupils – but however this may be I cannot say that I recollect with any degree of reverence or regard the worthy gentleman to whose direction Fate had consigned me. He was a burly, hard-featured – hardhanded – and as far as I know a somewhat hard-hearted Caledonian. The business of the School was conducted with great regularity, the customary discipline strictly maintained. The lessons were administered in due order – and it would be ungrateful to say that he neglected to perform his contract to teach as much as he could induce his pupils to learn of the several branches of instruction which he professed to impart to them. In reading, writing and arithmetic if they did not become proficient, it was their fault and not his. He had a smattering of schoolboy Latin; knew Cornelius Nepos – and Caesar's commentaries as well – perhaps better than his catechism – and had got so far in Ovid's *Metamorphoses* and the *Eclogues* of Virgil as enabled him to guide the construction and to render into vernacular prose the meaning of the text as well as he understood the meaning. Beyond such drudgery he had not a ray of intelligence. But he conducted his school satisfactorily – kept the boys to such work as they had to do – and provided them with sufficient though somewhat coarse food. He had a fixed belief that more than enough of beef and mutton – both very good – might cloud their intelligence but he never stinted them in boiled bacon and grey pease (things I thought were only fit for pigs). With a careful regard to their health, he dosed them regularly in each Spring and Fall of the year with brimstone and treacle. Mr. Dickens I believe has dilated upon this topic in his description of the treatment of the pupils at Dotheboys Hall – I forget the particular – but I can never forget the horror of trooping up, in file, to the brown Jorum in which the salutary medicine was contained, and from which it was handed out in a wooden spoon to each of the victims. At first it was unutterably nasty but after a little experience one got used to it – and I have no doubt, rough as the dose seemed to be, that it was as beneficial and served its purpose as well as any more elegant Exhibition that could be furnished by the Pharmacopaeia Londinensis. I should have mentioned that this dispensation was principally conducted by the Master's wife – a long severe-looking matron, who accompanied with a grimace which added to the infliction, and seemed to mock the patient as he bolted the nauseous compound.

There were several good ushers all of whom I believe were competent to supply the deficiencies of the Master. The one I best recollect was M. Le Capitaine, as he was called, who spared no pains in teaching us French – and who recompensed himself for the trouble he took with his most ungrateful scholars by bestowing upon their stupidity all the abusive epithets he could command in English – and a multitude of others in this own tongue, of which *cochon* was the most frequent and probably not the most offensive. Happily for us at least, our feelings were not wounded by the expletives and abuse which none of us understood. At all events he did make us somewhat acquainted with the French grammar, for which I am grateful to his memory.

I cannot say that I entertain any very agreeable recollections of my school days – but I do look back with great pleasure to them as being the period in which such intellect as God has given me began to expand – and when sense and knowledge, such as they were, and by such degrees as they came lightened up my understanding. There was a boy at the school, the son of a parson at Barnet, named Garrow, a brother of the famous Garrow, afterwards a judge, and then the most renowned professor of that most delicate and difficult art called cross-examination. I may have occasion to mention that learned judge hereafter. For the present I cannot refrain from expressing, *en passant*, my admiration for his talent in one of the most important and difficult branches in which the skill of an advocate can be displayed. This boy, Garrow, whom I have mentioned, brought with him to school from his father's library, some books of a kind far beyond anything I had any notion of. *Pilgrim's Progress* enraptured my soul – I could think of nothing else by day –and at night could not sleep without dreaming of it. I had before read some two-penny story of Robinson Crusoe – but now I had the full exuberant Defoe before me – never "while memory shall hold her seat in this distracted globe" can I forget the deep interest with which my soul was enthralled by the moving story. Besides these, Garrow, on his return from the holidays, brought *Roderic Random* and *Peregrine Pickle* and *Humphrey Clinker* and other books which woke me up to a new world. Men and things the existence of which I had before no knowledge or conception of, spread themselves out before me. I reveled in them — devoured, of course without understanding them, the marvelous creations of the mighty writers – and all the sources of imagination, fancy, and feeling that my mind was capable of brought into bright and warm activity.

I had been pushed and driven and had blundered through the dull task of endeavouring to make sense of Virgil's *Eclogues* without the slightest notion of what was meant. Garrow had brought a contraband volume of Dryden, which at once cleared up the dull clouds which had lowered over my desk – and I was able to understand what had before appeared to me (profane wretch that I was) dull and disgusting. For a time

Virgil was an object of veneration, almost of idolatry – but alas! The officers of justice detected the contraband article – the crib was discovered, impounded – the light was taken away and I was left to grope as well as I could – not however without a comfortable conviction the Sun did shine although its light was shut out from me.

My recollections of my schoolfellows are not very distinct. In general, I should say they were very much like the rest of mankind as I afterwards became acquainted with the race. Some few bright but mostly dull. A few lively and good-natured but the majority insipid – some careless, others stupid and sly. I remember one extravagant boy who mortgaged his week's pocket money for the present advance of three half pence, which he immediately laid out in the purchase of a red herring to be toasted over the flame of a tallow candle – I recollect the usurious lender who profited by the transaction. I wonder what became of them afterwards. If I were not writing a true history, a were at liberty to indulge my imagination, I could easily persuade myself that the borrower died in a workhouse – and that the lender became a Lord Mayor. There was one clever lively fellow Tom Munden, one of the big boys – in the upper class and some three or four years older than most of the others. He was the only son of a famous comic actor who for years was the delight of the playgoers of London. Charles Lamb has devoted some of his most pleasant pages to a critical essay on this artist. Of his merits of course I then could form no notion – but in after years I had often the delight of seeing him upon the – where he flourished to an advanced age – and sustained to the last the well-deserved praises which Charles Lamb has bestowed upon him – and was in all respects a most consummate artist. All I knew of him at the time I am now chronicling was that he lived in a most agreeable little villa within a quarter of a mile of our school, with a well stocked garden, the strawberries and gooseberries of which he allowed his son and his select companions (of whom I had the happiness to be one) to riot and revel in without stint. He was a most good-tempered, cheerful man and his wife was of the like kind. She had been an actress but had long retired from the stage – and amused herself by writing plays none of which I believe ever got beyond the state of manuscript. Poor Tom Munden was not fortunate in after life. He was placed in a merchant's office, where he had every reasonable prospect of prospering – he had acquired a good knowledge of modern languages – edited a translation in Portuguese of Pope's *An Essay on Man* made by a Portuguese customer of the firm – from which he derived no other advantage than some degree of empty praise. It was perhaps this exploit which induced him to give up commerce and betake himself to the Stock Exchange, where after some vicissitudes he was wholly ruined and the latter part of his life was passed in very straitened circumstances.

Another of my schoolfellows was poor Henry Neale, who was particularly recommended by his father to my care and protection. He was junior to me by several years, diminutive in stature, feeble in health, but of the sweetest temper and of intelligence far beyond his years. I left the school in about a year after I first made his acquaintance, but I afterwards knew him intimately up to the time of his most deplorable death.

Of public events of course schoolboys knew and thought very little – and cared less – but even in the region they inhabited such events as the deaths of Mr. Fox and Mr. Pitt, which happened at little distance from each other (Pitt January, and Fox September 1806) did create some sensation and it was at least understood even by boys that a great less had been sustained. The death of Nelson (1805) in the moment of victory, made a very distinct influence on the minds of all of us – and I especially remember that we had leave to go home for the purpose of witnessing the public funeral procession through the streets of London – and the countless crowds which were there collected to do honour to the memory of the hero.

How much I learned at school it would be difficult for me to guess – but this I know that I there acquired the habit of reading which has been the delight of my life and the means by which all such knowledge as I afterwards possessed was acquired. The world opened upon my tender mind – the beauties of nature dawned upon my soul – the character and pursuits of human beings became in some sense distinct, and the power of giving expression to the thoughts that crowded upon my understanding was to some extent acquired.

I was not twelve years old when, for some reason which I did not understand, I was removed from this school. Afterwards, for about a year, I was sent to a school at Pentonville, kept by a Mr. Darnell. I soon found that the change was by no means advantageous. The Master was a wholly incompetent person. The chief usher, an Irishman named Lawler, was, I believe, a scholar, but indolent and drunken in no small degree. The story went that he was a poet and that some of his works had been printed but I never saw any of them, and if I heard their titles, I have forgotten them. The French master was called M. L'Abbé Caron – an émigré Priest who was fortunate enough to see the restoration of Louis XVIII and, as I have heard, to be restored to the curacy in France from which he had been driven by the Revolution. He was a harmless, more than half-starved old man, gentle and stupid, and confined his instruction to hammering the accidence of the French grammar into the thick heads of the boys. I was conceited enough to think that I knew already more than I had any opportunity of learning from my new instructors – and I suppose I represented this to my father so strongly as to induce him to withdraw me from this unprofitable school.

Among the pupils was John, the eldest son of Charles Dibdin the Younger, to distinguish him from his father, the deservedly celebrated author of *The Sea Songs*. This second Charles Dibdin was then the manager and poet of Sadler's Wells Theatre. My father and he had formerly been intimate friends. Some differences (I never knew what) had estranged them – but John Dibdin, who was just about my age, became my most intimate crony and we were greatly attached to each other during the rest of his life, which was terminated by consumption in his 20th year. He was as good a man as I have ever met with. I also became acquainted with his father and his family, and although the old friendship never regained its former footing they remained upon civil speaking terms.

First Employment

I had now gained the ripe age of twelve years and a half. It was supposed that I could be employed in some sort of business, and the circumstances of the family seemed to require that I should at least be no longer a burden to the common interest.

My father had at this time formed an engagement with a long-established firm of attorneys in Clerkenwell as the manager of their in-door business. They had carried on for many years, and with considerable profit and great reputation, the affairs of the County attorneys as their Agents. It was at that time absolutely indispensable that the County practitioners should have correspondents in London by whom the practical details which the County attorneys were ignorant of, and which by reason of the distances, and for other reasons, they were wholly incompetent to deal with. And thus, upon an understanding that the clear profits should be divided, the London attorneys did in fact perform all the operative parts of the practice – often advancing the greater part of the capital for fees and other necessary disbursements. This business had, as I understood, been established many years before by Mr. Abraham Rhodes – now a man of more than 80 years old. Besides this agency business, the firm had acquired clients whose affairs were often of great importance and highly lucrative. They were the professional managers of the large estates of Lord Downshire in Ireland and also in England – of Bilson Legge, Chancellor of the Exchequer and of his descendants, and of many other noblemen and gentlemen owners of large landed possessions, and the transactions with which were highly profitable. The agency business was under the control of Mr. William Cook, whose knowledge of common law practice, and more than that, whose activity and spirited enterprise qualified him admirably for the task, while it left the not less important but more tranquil business relating to the estates and affaires of the landed proprietors to the care of Mr. Rhodes. While that gentleman was able to give the requisite attention to this last mentioned department, all seems to have gone on most satisfactorily. But his advancing years, and his consequent infirmities, had rendered necessary some serviceable assistance which Mr. Cook was neither inclined nor perhaps competent to afford. And thus it was that in an evil hour for the prosperity of the concern the two partners, Rhodes and Cook admitted into their partnership Mr. Handley – a man much younger than either of them – who had been for many years one of their managing clerks and who displayed such ability and energy as seemed to qualify him admirably for supplying the exertions requisite to maintain the reputation and prosperity of the concern. The firm became Rhodes, Cook and Handley – and for several years I believe that it stood high among the practitioners of London. What circumstances may have led to the changes which ensued I cannot tell – who was to blame for those changes is unknown to me – but the facts were plain enough. Mr. Handley succeeded in attracting to himself all the most valuable, because the most lucrative, part of the business – that relating to the estates and affairs of the noble and distinguished and most wealthy of the clients proper, - conducted those affairs in a separate establishment of his own in his private house at Pentonville – never showed his face in the offices of the firm at Clerkenwell and took no part in the conduct of the business there carried on. I suppose the elder partners were dissatisfied – probably alarmed at the state of things – the partnership term had yet several years to run – Rhodes and Cook determined to endeavour to retrieve the mistake they had made. Under these circumstances it was that they proposed and my father accepted that he should become the manager of the Clerkenwell business – that is to say – so much of it as Mr. Handley had not effectually transferred to his own personal and immediate conduct at Pentonville.

I thereupon was entered as a clerk – with no other qualification than that I could write a tolerably good hand and was admittedly young enough to learn whatever anybody would take the trouble to teach me. And thus I began to learn what the world was made of and by what kind of beings it was inhabited. I can't say that anybody took much trouble to teach me anything – but I had unlimited opportunities of trying to teach myself – and by degrees, sometimes slow and often obscure. I did by dint of experience and observation become acquainted with many men and things by which my subsequent progress in the world was directed.

Young as I was, I had read an abundance of things – I had devoured much poetry – my soul had been often thrilled with the force and beauty of verse of the real weight and worth of which I had no adequate understanding but which yet had afforded me inexpressible delight. I knew the stories as told and the personages as described by Smollett and Defoe and Fielding and Swift – but the impressions they had made upon me were dim and lifeless. I had exulted at the Mafic Lanthorn Exhibition which were displayed before me, but they remained to me creatures of the imagination only. Now it was my lot to see the things and men in *the flesh* – to hear their speech, to mark their actions, and to learn and know as well as I could the difference between the ideal phantoms and the rough and solid reality.

We left Somers Town and occupied a house in Brayne's Row Spa Fields – a row of houses extending from the prison (Middlesex House of Correction, familiarly and reproachfully called the Bastille) eastward to St. John Street – and fronting upon wide open fields reaching to the height of Pentonville. A few scattered buildings – a public house of some notoriety call "Merlin's Cave" and the Reservoir and Water works of the New River Company were the only structures upon the extensive space before us which was principally occupied by the wooden pipes by which the water was supplied to the several mains in the streets lying to the westward. These fields were afterwards, and not unfrequently, the scene of radical and seditious assemblages headed by the demagogues of those days – Orator Hurst of the White Hat, Dr. Watson, Thistlewood, and other dangerous rebels. Out of the meetings there held grew the formidable Corn Law Riots and the most striking and desperate – the Cato Street Conspiracy – and several of the most noted of the scoundrels who figured here were afterwards brought to justice and expiated their crimes against the public peace upon the scaffold.

In the meantime and for several years all was quiet enough – the site was pleasant and healthy and the walks across the fields agreeable; the only drawback was a dismal burial ground (only visible from the upper rooms in the rear of our house) which was principally devoted, because of its small charges, to the poorer classes. The rest of Clerkenwell was inhabited by a numerous population of industrious artisans employed in the various branches of the watchmaking trade, most of whom worked at home in the garrets of sheds belonging to the houses.

The general appearance of the parish was that of a suburb to the great city. Now and for many years past, all this has been changed. The green fields have wholly disappeared, and every practicable foot of ground has been covered by buildings – streets and rows of houses spread over the whole of the surface and Spa Fields are fields no more. The wooden pipes have been superseded by iron ones – which have descended into lower regions and have disappeared from mortal sight. Pentonville and Islington, formerly neighbouring villages, have joined hands with Clerkenwell – they form one map and Sadler's Wells once isolated and flourishing on the bank of the Open New River is now jammed in between them.

The head of the concern into which I was thus introduced was Mr. Abraham Rhodes – a very old man who had long relinquished any very active exertions – but who still employed himself to some extent in the correspondence with the County solicitors and in some matters of mere superintendence. He was a tall man of severe aspect dressed in a suit of iron-grey – breeches and black worsted stockings, steel cut buckles in his shoes – and a formidable walking stick. He occupied the original building in which the business had been established. A low, two-storied house, at the eastern end of which extensive offices had been from time to time added. He had been greatly interested in antiquarian pursuits and I believe enjoyed a reputation in the Society of Antiquaries. At one time he had contemplated a history of the parish of Clerkenwell, and with this view had made a large collection of monumental inscriptions from the old Church – all carefully stored in several large chests where they shared the doom of other good intentions never to be accomplished.

He had besides a very extensive collection of books, some of great rarity and value of which I only knew some of the titles, as they could be read through the glass doors of the carefully locked bookcases which filled the upper floor of the house. Their own merit and the old man's reputation must have been considerable, for they fetched and an auction by Sotheby more than £2,000 after his death. His household consisted of this grandson – the son of his only child, who was Mr. Cook's first wife, and who had died several years before. This young man who had been always educated by Mr. Rhodes, was 8 years older than I and soon became my intimate companion. The domestic affairs were conducted by a fierce old duenna, called Mrs. Springfield, who reigned supreme and was held in awe by all comers. My first occupation consisted in copying letters and writing from the dictation of the old gentleman – and in what was called examining deeds etc., which had been prepared for execution – that is I read the drafts aloud and the old gentleman saw that the engrossments were accurately copied. I suppose that by this exercise I must have acquired some knowledge of the phraseology of the things dealt with but certainly without any approach to understanding them. The old gentleman was not morose, or in any degree unkind – but he was not at all communicative, and I don't recollect that my ideas, such as they were, were either improved or extended by my intercourse with him. He quitted his home only to walk to a quiet public house at the end of Rosoman Street where at seven o'clock every evening he drank a glass of Negus – smoked a pipe filled with stramonium – supposed to be "the sov'ranest thing on earth" for the asthma with which he was grievously troubled – and read the newspaper of the day – and at nine he returned home and to bed.

But although Mr. Rhodes's name stood first in the firm – his pre-eminence was merely nominal. The real active spirit was Mr. Cook. It was his energy which sustained the prosperity of the concern. His knowledge of all parochial operations – his industry and application had sustained it for several years after Mr. Rhodes's years and infirmity had disqualified him from the exertions necessary of its maintenance. Besides the merely professional business he had attracted numerous clients among the stirring commercial persons of the neighbourhood and elsewhere. He was appointed the Vestry Clerk of the parish and the Clerk to the Commissioners of Pavements, a body constituted under a local Act of Parliament. These two offices involved multifarious and even important duties, all of which were admirably discharged by Mr. Cook – and he had as fair a prospect of acquiring a considerable fortune by his own personal exertions as could be desired, when a circumstance happened which, apparently highly beneficial, turned out by what is called the irony of fate to be a real lasting calamity.

At the end of the street in which the offices stood there was a considerable space of ground, reaching eastward to St. John Street. Upon a part of this was a large old house and out-buildings occupied by a Mr. Friend, who there carried on a very extensive business as a dyer, his principal employers being the East India Company – then in their highest prosperity and importance, and his operations consisting of dyeing the cloths required for the troops in their service. In this calling Mr. Friend had acquired a large fortune. He was without children or any near relation. He had a wife from whom he was separated by reason of her misconduct and to whom he paid some inconsiderable alimony. He formed a strong attachment for Mr. Cook and his family – and after several years of close and cordial intimacy he by will left to Mr. Cook the whole of his property. All this, of course, I know only by what has been told me. He died several years before I was acquainted with Mr. Cook and before the occurrence of the events I am about to state.

The very considerable space of ground upon which the house – workshops and out-buildings – stood where held of the Trustees of the Charter House under the will of Sutton, the Founder of that Charity, upon a lease about to expire. Mr. Cook unfortunately for himself conceived the notion of pulling down the existing buildings and erecting a handsome and commodious structure upon the site – and with this view entered int negotiations with the Trustees who were then resident at Woodbridge in Suffolk through their attorney living at that place and it was at length agreed that the existing lease should be surrendered and a new one granted on condition that Mr. Cook should expend a very large sum of money and pay an increased rent. It was unquestionably the belief of Mr. Cook and the intention of the then Trustees, that the lease should be subject to renewal upon reasonable terms. Unfortunately (and as it now appears to me -inexplicable) this stipulation was not mentioned in the new lease. The new house was built at a cost of several thousand pounds – with the sanction and approval of the Trustees and their Architect – and under the inspection of a Mr. Spiller an architect of eminence in London employed by Mr. Cook and was far too large and too good for the place in which it was situated. Upon his application for a renewal of his lease, the Trustees denied their liability to grant a new lease and ultimately resumed possession of Woodbridge House, by which proceeding Mr. Cook lost the large sums he had expended. By the sudden accession to wealth his habits of order and economy were wholly disturbed. He bought a house and grounds and some acres of land at Clay Hill Enfield and spent much more than was prudent in making it a most agreeable summer residence with extensive gardens, and in several other enterprises which were never clearly explained. In the course of not many years there came to an end not only the East India stock, which he had derived under the will of Mr. Friend – but also all the money he could command, and he had besides contracted a large amount of debt which he had not the means of satisfying. Besides his pecuniary losses, his attention to business was relaxed to a most injurious extent. The clients took their business elsewhere. The public offices which he had filled, and which were

annually renewed, were given to competitors – and he was compelled to
retire to the Continent with such diminished means as he could manage to
collect.

      Before this catastrophe, there could not have been a happier or
more orderly family than this. He kept no carriage – never more than two
horses – which he drove in a green cart alternately in his too frequent visits
to Clay Hill. Mrs. Cook was clever in all respects – she had been educated
at Lille and well educated. Good governesses were supplied for the
children – music was very sedulously cultivated. Old Mr. Horn, a German,
the father of Charles Horn (of the song "Cherry Ripe") who was then a
popular composer – superintended the musical studies. The family
consisted of four daughters and one son – and another daughter was added
after a considerable interval. The eldest daughter married a Mr. Crickett,
a proctor. The second, Laura, it was afterward my supreme happiness to
call my wife – my guardian angel! – the source of all the real happiness of
my life, whose name I cannot write, of whom I can never think without
deep, inconsolable grief. Elizabeth, the third daughter, afterwards married
the Count Szeliski – a Pole who had served with distinction in Bonaparte's
Grande Armée. Emma, the last-born, married to Mr. Scott, then an
employee in the Treasury and who carried her abroad upon his being
appointed Lieutenant-Governor of Labuan and Natal [and later Governor
of British Guiana] – and Robert, the only son, – who became one of the
staff of the Ecclesiastical Commissioners and has recently died. Scott was
knighted after many years of diplomatic service – in several colonial
governments – and, his wife having died very suddenly about two years
ago, Sir John Scott is living in ease and retirement at East Finchley.

Laura and friendships

I cannot trust myself to attempt to describe the happiness that I enjoyed in
the society of this family before the misfortunes I have alluded to arrived.
My mind was gradually opened, a taste for refined pleasures was formed.
New prospects – ardent aspirations were created – but above all the
purifying influence of the passion for Laura which had taken possession
of my soul became the very spirit and governing power of my life.

(I have traced very imperfectly and without regard to chronology – the state of the family of which I became in fact a member – and I now return to the history – such as it is – of my own personal proceedings. The preceding pages being a digression from that history but containing a narrative indispensably necessary. It must borne in mind that the work has been carried on irregularly – subject to many interruptions – and occasionally by fits and starts.)

By degrees I became, I suppose, more useful. The intercourse with the clerks employed in the establishment of course increased my knowledge upon a great variety of subjects and quickened my understanding without, however, any great improvement in my moral perceptions. I began to see how men acted and could not help learning how they talked. I do not think they were, any of them, estimable persons. The most remarkable among them was the managing clerk, who was called Johnson – a very good-looking clever fellow, master of his business – full of good spirits – but unfortunately for himself addicted to pursuits not compatible with the drudgery of his calling. His salary was by no means adequate to his expenses – and he was tempted to endeavour to supply the deficiency by means of gaming. There were then, as there are now, many hells at the West End of the Town. At one of these, where play from very low to very high stakes was encouraged, this poor Johnson was induced to risk not only all he had – including of course his earlier winnings (for at first it was said his good luck was very remarkable) but considerable sums with which he had been entrusted for the purposes of the business and other moneys which he had contrived to get into his hands by interrupting country letters containing enclosures – and occasionally forging the signatures to drafts and bills. Upon the discovery of his offence, he was arrested and imprisoned, made a full confession of his delinquency, and of all the circumstances connected with it. Legal proceedings were taken against the proprietors of the gaming house, and in the result I believe the whole amount of which the firm had been defrauded was recovered. What became of Johnson *then* I do not know, but I know that several years afterwards he was living without discredit and was acting as managing clerk to a firm of solicitors in London. The hell continued its practices.

Two Jews and an attorney named Fielder were the proprietors and the general report was that they all made a good deal of money by it.

The other clerks were chiefly copyists, with the exception of one prim, formal old man, to whom the care of the books was committed. He was a model of propriety and from him I learned some of the mysteries of bookkeeping, which I have found very useful and for which I am thankful.

Courts of Law

From these two men, I picked up insensibly scraps of knowledge which as I grew older became so valuable that as the years rolled on I was employed in a multitude of small affairs by which I was rescued from the dull toil of copying at the desk – sent about to the common law offices – became acquainted with the names and shapes of writs, declarations, pleas, etc., and was entrusted with the service of proofs and sent to watch the progress of such business as was conducted in the courts. Thus I remember the Court of Chancery in Lincoln's Inn Old Hall when Lord Eldon presided there and have seen Sir William Grant sitting in his armchair at the Rolls – while the leaders there sat in front of him upon wide horsehair chairs – the outer bar being deposited upon benches behind them.

Lincoln's Inn Hall was the brighter and more striking of these scenes. Lord Eldon's approach was announced by the appearance of the Mace Bearer and the man carrying the Great Seal in the purse – who were followed by the solemn functionary called Chaff-wax. Two Masters in Chancery preceded the Chancellor and took their seats on low benches on either side of him. He then took possession of a capacious armchair, with a small round table at his side, upon which lay such papers as he might have occasion for, together with a superb bouquet of fresh flowers. The Registrars sat at the table, and in front of them was spread a large plateau also containing fresh flowers. The Chancellor then called upon the Senior Counsel to move (I am now telling of a Seal-day) and on his beginning – the Chancellor nodded to the two masters. They then rose, bowed to the Lord Chancellor and retired to their chambers. The business at the Court then went on, not at all interrupted by the habit which the Chancellor had of writing letters on paper which he held in the palm of his hand. If he wanted, as he hardly ever did, to take a note it was done in the same manner. In those days no Judge ever wrote upon a desk or table, or in a notebook.

Sir William Grant's appearance was much the same – but he had no other officers accompanying him but his Secretary and the Registrar and I don't recollect that he had any flowers – probably because his sitting commenced at seven in the evening, when the flowers would be no longer fresh. The sitting at the Rolls was so quiet that you might fancy you were in Church. Whether all this was better than the existing state of things is not worth considering – but it is because it was so different that I here mention it.

The Lord Chancellor sat at Westminster during the Terms. The Court of Chancery there was at the South End of Hall on the West Side and separated from the Courts of King's Bench by a broad flight of stone steps leading to the passages to the Houses of Lords and Commons. I have been frequently in both of these Courts. In the Common Law Court, I was present at the remarkable case of an appeal of murder brought by the heir of the murdered woman against the alleged murderer who had been acquitted at his previous trial at the Assizes. The case excited very great interest as well from the circumstances of the proceeding being of most rare occurrence as from the general suspicion that the person accused was really guilty. All the particulars (which are well worth reading) may be found in the State Trials. In this Court Lord Ellenborough was sitting as Chief Justice – Garrow and Bayley were there also.

Besides such acquaintance as I thus made with the Courts of Common Law and Equity, I was introduced to the practice of the Court of the Middlesex Sessions held at Hick's Hall on Clerkenwell Green. Mr. Cook held the office of Vestry Clerk of the Parish – and was also Clerk to the board of Guardians of Clerkenwell. Indictments for nuisances and for small misdemeanours were not infrequent – but there was besides a more important branch of business consisting of appeals under the then existing Poor Law against the orders of the magistrates relating to the Settlement of Paupers. The burden of maintaining paupers was often so heavy as to induce parishes to fight the question of their liability – and questions of fast and the points of law arising out of them made the subjects highly interesting. At the same time, the serious point of costs made it worth the while of legal practitioners to have these matters discussed with due solemnity. Old Mr. (with Mr. Const (whom in after years I became very well acquainted) was a most efficient Chairman, – the Bar was very well supplied – Mr. Adolphus a very eloquent and able advocate and a man of undeniable talent was one of the leaders – Mr. Alley and Sergeants Andrew and Adams (Jack Adams) and many other promising juniors frequented this Court. The last named became afterwards Chairman of the Middlesex Sessions and was the father of that Adams who has lately distinguished himself in his quarrels with [Attorney General of England John Duke] Coleridge whose daughter Adams married. I believe that my experience in the pursuits I have mentioned taught me much and indeed much more useful and valuable practical knowledge than I could have gained by any other more serious and less desultory course of study.

Besides the offices I have mentioned, Mr. Cook was Clerk to the Commissioners for Pavements of the Parish – constituted under a Local Act of Parliament. This board consisted of some score or more of the most renowned tradesmen of the district – I forget what their requisite qualification was – but they were all reported to be and were in good circumstances and generally intelligent and men of business. Their meetings were held fortnightly. They assessed the rates which they were empowered to collect and enforce their payment. They entered into contracts for paving and lighting and watching the streets – and employed officers to inspect and protect the several ways from all nuisances and encroachments. Now all these duties could not be discharged without much care and attention and often after due deliberation. Many serious discussions ensued at their little fortnightly parliaments. Differences of opinion sometimes occurred – but the debates were always carried on with due decorum – and with regard to the rights and welfare of the inhabitants. Some inconsiderate persons did sometimes complain that the little occasional dinners which the Commissioners had – and which they found necessary for the proper discharge of their multifarious and onerous duties – ought not to have been paid for out of the rates – but such complaints were not encouraged by the right-minded majority of the inhabitants, and I am bound to say that there was nothing like extravagance in the application of the public money – not the slightest tinge of jobbery on the part of the Commissioners. It soon became my exclusive duty to attend the meeting of the Board – to record their debates, to frame their resolutions – and to see they were duly reported and executed – all of which was done as I believe to the general satisfaction of all parties concerned.

In these employments I continued without finding them very burdensome, although the greater part of them were not of a nature to move or interest me much. I was approaching manhood and some instinct suggested to me that I might aim at some more distinguished occupation. I had been articled to Mr. Cook with a view to my admission as an attorney – but the distant future which that presented was not very cheerful – and it was not possible for me to conceal from myself that the general business of the concern was for reasons I may explain more fully elsewhere in a state of decay. I don't remember that I thought very deeply on this subject – I found plenty of time for other pursuits.

Society

My home was pleasant, and although our means did not enable any of us to enjoy any great variety of amusements we were not discontented. My love of reading afforded me always great satisfaction. The circulating library in Leather Lane brought most of the new books within my reach. Scott and Moore and Byron were familiar sources of delight and in my twentieth year – as well as I recollect – I became acquainted with Dr. Evans and his family – a circumstance which greatly influenced by future career. My friend John Dibdin had introduced me to his father – and he had given me a free admission to Sadler's Wells Theatre – a privilege of which I availed myself – not too frequently but very much to my amusement. What I valued much more was the pleasant conversation and encouragement of the father and the companionship of his sons John and Charles and his daughter Mary. John was employed as a clerk to a firm of Manchester Warehouse in Cheapside – Charles who displayed taste and skill in art had become the pupil of John Wilson, a marine Painter of some celebrity, and who then filled the post of Scene Painter at the Surrey Theatre. Mary Dibdin who was of my own age, had been educated as a musician and had profited so much under the instruction of Mr. Chatterton, and afterwards of Signor Bochea, as to have established her reputation as a performer on the harp, then a most fashionable instrument much cultivated by young ladies. By occasional playing at concerts, but much more by giving lessons at Ladies' Schools, Mary Dibdin had secured a quasi-independent position. The manager's means were by no means affluent. The theatre was often out at elbows in spite of the attractions of the popular Clown Grimaldi, and its gains at best so moderate that the contributions which Mary Dibdin was enabled to make to the common stock were of substantial advantage. Still the home there was a very happy one, – and all its inmates were good and amiable people. The years that have elapsed have not dimmed my recollection of the many happy hours I have passed in their society.

Doctor Evans kept a school at Islington for a limited number of pupils, all the sons of persons of means who could afford to pay more than the ordinary rate of charges at boys' boarding schools. He was held in great esteem by the dissenting portions of the community – and was the author of a very popular history of all the denominations of religious dissent. His school had been long established – he had been so prosperous that he had been able to accumulate a handsome independency, and had obtained the honour of a Doctor's Degree from the American University of Rhode Island. I believe that he was rather proud of this distinction. He had, when I first knew him, lost the use of his lower limbs and was carried by his affectionate sons whenever he had to change his place. He continued to superintend his school, and to conduct the service of his church in Worship Street, Moorfields, where he preached admirable sermons to within a short period before his death. His designation in the sect of dissent to which he was attached was that of Arian Baptist. I cannot say that I know distinctly all or what that means but I do know that he was a pious Christian, a man of extensive knowledge – an honourable, generous, cheerful gentleman – a beloved and honoured by all who were so fortunate as to know him. Of all the men I have known, I have met with no one more deserving of unqualified esteem, or whose memory is more dear to me than that of Dr. Evans.

His family consisted of his wife, a most kind, gentle, clever woman – and four sons. John, who had been educated at Edinburgh, where he had been worthily distinguished for his proficiency in mathematics, and who afterwards became a barrister practicing in the Court of Chancery. Hugh, then articled to an attorney in Gray's Inn and who became my most intimate friend, of whom I shall have much more to say. Caleb, who was educated for the ministry in his father's Church and who died in his 24th year – and George, who was then a boy of about 15 years old – who afterwards was called to the bar and went to America, where he died.

Two o'clock on Sunday was the dinner hour – the school dinner. Roast beef and plumb pudding the unchangeable fare. For several years, I shared in this dinner. The afternoons commonly spent in long walks with the sons and other guests of whom there were many. I here became acquainted with many excellent persons of whom I have to mention two specially. Benjamin and John Bell – both principal clerks in the house of Jeremiah Harman & Co., then eminent, if not the most eminent merchants in the City of London. They, the Bells, were men of great knowledge – acquainted with all the public affairs of Europe – both admirable linguists conducting the correspondence with France, Germany, Italy and Spain – and from my commerce with them I acquired knowledge of various kinds which I have found to be very beneficial upon many occasions. Indeed it was, I think, principally under the influence of their example that I turned my attention to the acquisition of modern languages. I knew *some* French and endeavoured assiduously to extend that knowledge in which they gave me very valuable assistance. Besides becoming acquainted with some of the best masters of French literature, I studied Italian with the help of a very poor Italian gentleman who had been driven by the political troubles of his country to seek a refuge here. With great difficulty and at great risk, he had managed to escape the fate which befell many of his brother *carbonari*.[1] He was a scholar and a gentleman. How he managed to exist here I do not know – but I believe he was reduced to the utmost straits – and was not unwilling to help me to read Ariosto and Tasso for the very inadequate remuneration of 1/6 an hour. After a couple of months, he disappeared and I never knew what became of him. So I continued to spell on, as well as I could, but all the better for such assistance as he had rendered me.

---

[1] Italian rebels of the 1820s.

First scribblings

At the same time, I was completely restless. With a strong desire to do something of which I could earn money – for the narrowness of our circumstances was the only real evil of which I could complain, I cast about for the means of satisfying that most natural and not blameable desire. My home was comfortable enough. My parents kind and indulgent – I had many pleasant companions, my pursuits were agreeable and innocent – but I felt that I was so hedged in that I must do something to satisfy my craving for the enjoyment which money alone could procure. I naturally and necessarily turned to literature as the only means by which that craving could be satisfied. My friend John Dibdin had formed an acquaintance with a bookseller in Cornhill (Letts) who was the proprietor and publisher of a monthly magazine called *The European*, a publication of small repute, which existed rather upon such small circulation as remained of its former prosperity. It was edited by a Mr. Thompson, a seedsman in Fenchurch Street, who possessed no other qualification for the office he had undertaken than a love of scribbling and great industry. The advertisements and reviews by the booksellers were the only means by which the magazine was kept alive. The only writers in it were the seedsman, and his brother who had a small post in the Mint, and who indulged his antiquarian propensities by treatises upon the records of the Tower and other interesting remains of Old London. Through John Dibdin, I was introduced to this editor, and by his permission some articles which I had written were inserted. Whatever their merit (if they had any) may have been there was no thought of payment for them – and gratified as I was at seeing myself in print I did not by these exertions find myself any nearer to the object I had in view. The exercise was, however, useful. I acquired the knack of stringing sentences together, and obtained a certain facility of expression which encouraged me to make further exertions.

I have taxed my memory – but wholly without success – to recall the circumstances under which I became acquainted with Mr. John Robins, who with his brother Joseph carried on the business of printers in Ivy Lane Paternoster Row. They had a somewhat extensive trade in books and especially such as were published in sixpenny numbers. Among these was a "pocket magazine." I was somehow invited to contribute to this, and

wrote many tales, essays, criticisms, and some poetry for which I was paid
– not largely – but to an extent which made me for the first time owner of
money from the fruit of my own earnings and with which I was pleased,
and I daresay somewhat proud. There appeared at about this time several
romantic novels in French. The great masters in the art had not then
appeared – Balzac, Dumas, Sue. And the other writers who shed such
brilliant light upon the romantic narrative branch of French literature were
yet to come – but a certain Vicomte d'Arlincourt had produced some
romances which attained a certain notoriety. My new patrons the Robinses
agreed with me for a translation of *Le Renegat* in 2 small volumes for
which they paid me the sum of twenty pounds. I set about this task with
infinite satisfaction and dispatched it with at least great industry. As well
as I recollect, it was about equal in merit to the ordinary productions of the
Minerva Press – but it was rather novel in its character and style. It was to
some extent successful – so much so that the publishers were induced not
long afterwards to undertake the Vicomte's succeeding novel, *Ipsiboe*,
which I translated on the same terms and with like success. Encouraged
by this attempt, I began to feel my legs and persuaded myself that there
was at least a probability that I might make a livelihood by my pen. I
performed a great variety of scribbling of all sorts – helped other labourers
in the same field who had undertaken more than they could perform and
shared with them such wages as the publishers paid. I cannot recollect (and
if I could it would not be worth recording) the kinds and quantities of stuff
on which I was engaged – but I do know that I worked very hard and that
my labours, though not light, were not disagreeable. Among other things,
I helped poor Graham to translate the memoirs of the old Duchess of
Orleans – the mother of the Regent, and some other of his numerous works
– all of which were rather better paid for by Whitaker a publisher of higher
degree in the trade than my earlier patrons the Robinses.

Graham's fate was remarkable. He was born in the United States
– and had displayed from his earliest years very remarkable talents and
had obtained an important and lucrative post in a great commercial
establishment in New York. A love of pleasure and the flattery which
accompanied his career, acting upon a very irregular condition of mind,
soon led him into extravagant habits. Born a gamester – madly addicted to

play – he soon fell a victim to his weak and vicious propensities, and would have suffered perhaps an extreme penalty, but for the forbearance and compassion of his employers – who were said to have permitted, if they did not connive at, his escape from America. He fled to Europe and for some years lived – no one knew how – in France and Germany. All I knew of this I learned from Jenny Russell – who had encountered him in Germany, – and who knew him then to be a *habitué* of the gaming tables there. Upon his coming to England, he became connected with newspaper editors. His acquirements as a linguist – his almost universal talents, his great readiness with his pen and his good looks and engaging manners soon made him a universal favorite. He got into good company in the literary and theatrical world, earned with great facility an abundantly sufficient income and might easily have escaped recognition – but that the demon of play held him in thrall. There was no fear of his being pursued in England by the persons he had wronged in America – and his previous history was wholly unknown by those with those with whom he associated in England. In his capacity of drama critic, one of his many literary occupations, he was free of [charge at] all theatres. In the lobby of Drury Lane Theatre, he found himself face to face with Stephen Price, an American and then connected with the theatre, of which he shortly afterwards became the manager. Graham disengaged himself from the merry companions with whom he had been conversing and approached Price, whom he drew aside and said, "Mr. Price, I once had the honour of knowing you – and I am aware that you know me and all about me. Some years have since elapsed. What I have suffered I need not tell you – but I have endeavoured to retrieve my past offences. I have established a reputation and the means of living in credit and propriety in England. I am aware that it is in your power by disclosing all you know of me, to destroy all my present prospects and to bring me to utter ruin." "Sir," said Price, interrupting him, "I request you not to say anything more to me now – and not to speak to me on any other occasion – and nobody shall know from me that I ever set eyes on you before." He then turned away and although they must have frequently been in the presence of each other, nobody knew until after Graham's death that they had known each other.

Graham remained in London a good while after this. His love of play overcame all his good resolves if he made any. Loaded with debt, and penniless, he raised money by forging the acceptance of Whitaker to some bills of exchange. A warrant was issued for his apprehension. The means of flight were raised, not without difficulty, from friends who were almost as poor as himself and among others Pat Murphy, the father of the present Q.C., pawned his favorite and valuable flute and gave the proceeds to the fugitive. He escaped to America – picked a quarrel at a gaming table with a celebrated duelist – went out, and was shot dead on the field!

Among the numerous scribbling exploits in which I was engaged was one which was very near getting us into trouble. The death of Lord Byron had occasioned a profound sensation in the reading public. My enterprising publisher (Robins) conceived the notion that it would be a good opportunity for bringing out a memoir and a descriptive criticism of the noble poet's works – to be published in numbers – and illustrated by wood engravings designed by George Cruickshank. We accordingly set to work. The scissors and paste pot were exercised very actively – the original portion (if such a phrase may be used) I furnished – and I believe the work which, when completed, formed a good-sized octave volume was proceeding satisfactorily when Mr. Murray became dissatisfied at the extensive use which was made of Byron's works, of which he owned the copyright. A thunderbolt fell on the printing office in the shape of a threatening letter from Murray's solicitor.

It was determined in a council of war to put as good a face upon the matter as possible, and the lawyer's letter was replied to with great civility – but insisting at the same time upon the right of discussing the poet's merits, etc., and the impossibility of exercising that right without making copious extracts from the works themselves, – and protesting against the notion that so harmless a work as ours could interfere with the property of Mr. Murray. Whether he was convinced by this reasoning – or reluctant to run the risk of litigation after the ill-luck which had attended the recent piracy of Don Juan – and the doubts which had been suggested as to the legal right which existed in literary productions of questionable morality I am unable to assert – but it is certain that no further steps were taken by Murray and our book was carried to its conclusion with good profit of which my share was not considerable.

I got more money – I forget how much – by translating a dreadful romance of Victor Hugo's called *Han d'Islande* – the first of a long series of works by which he afterwards became famous. It was in preparing this that I first became acquainted with Cruikshank. He executed some very admirable etchings for this publication. He was mightily taken with the story. We had many very pleasant discussions about the passages to be illustrated – I watch with great interest the operations upon the copper – and I thought then, and I think still that among his innumerable productions none are more admirable for invention and skill in execution than these. His reputation as an artist is so well established – his originality, genius and ability so universally recognized that I need say nothing about them – but I cannot forbear to say that although he was somewhat eccentric he was as honourable and upright and manly a person as I have ever known. I have a very distinct and pleasant recollection of the dinners we have had in the publisher's back parlour in Ivy Lane – not splendid nor very luxurious – a leg of mutton cooked at the baker's, with potatoes browned and soft filling the bottom of the dish, porter and toasted cheese – and the repast crowned with gin and water in moderation and not without tobacco. Mirth, good humour and light hearts enabled us to pass the evening – (we never dined till after the day's work was done) without envying the Lord Mayor or any other potentate. For sixty years or thereabouts I was well acquainted with Cruikshank, who died only about 2 years ago. He taught me to etch on copper, but I am afraid I did not profit much by his instruction. He became colonel of a regiment of volunteers and in the later years of his life (renouncing the gin and water of Ivy Lane and all other spiritous liquors) became a total abstainer.

Travels

In the spring of 1822, I resolved to indulge the longing by which I was possessed of seeing something beyond the Channel. I had no engagements to prevent me – the law business had dwindled to nothing – and I had money enough to enable me with great frugality to wander abroad for three weeks. Neale, who had already departed, proposed that I should join him in Paris and it was determined that we should visit Switzerland together and go as far as our means (his were no better than mine) would enable us. A steamboat carried me from the Tower to Calais in a long summer day – the weather being all that could be wished for and I – bad sailor as I was, suffering little from the voyage. It would be impossible for me to describe the pleasure which I derived from my first steps on the French soil. All was new and delightful. The fisherwomen with their white short petticoats and sabots I thought charming – I looked in vain for Hogarth's *Gate of Calais* – but I saw the port which Turner's picture had made familiar to me. I paid a devout visit to Dessin's Hotel, and venerated the room in which Sterne received the visit of the Franciscan Monks.

At the end of the garden there was a small theatre in which I learnt the full meaning of parterre – for the floor of what we call the pit was without bench or seat of any kind and the audience stood literally *par terre*. Do not imagine that I put up at Dessin's – that was far beyond my means – but I lodged satisfactorily enough at an inferior though very respectable hotel in one of the side streets leading from the marketplace, ate such a supper as the *table d'hôte* afforded, and was lulled to sleep by the ever cheerful carillon from the grotesque and ugly befoul. The diligence to Paris did not start till the evening of the next day, so I employed my time in studying the humour of the market-place, visiting the harbor and the ramparts and inspecting the people all of which were so pleasing to my inexperienced eyes as to fill me with delight. I mounted the diligence – there was yet enough of daylight to enable me to see the country till we had got some distance beyond Boulogne. After that I slept soundly enough – not unthankful for the ample rough capote which the merry conductor lent me.

I remember being struck by the massive towers of the Churches at Abbeville and Beauvais, but in general the road presented nothing of interest – the pace was tiresome – and the conversation of the old soldier (one of Napoleon's veterans) not always intelligible to me soon lost its charm. I indemnified myself as well as I could by sleeping on the hard but not uneasy banquette. It was night of the next day before we reached Paris. A fiacre carried me and my luggage – which consisted only of a travelling bag to the hotel in the Faubourg Poissonière to which I had been directed, where I found Neale. We stayed only two days in Paris. They were spent in perambulating the streets, in staring at the exterior of the Louvre – the Hotel de Ville, the Tuilleries, the quays etc., and having had our passports visés (a matter then of most rigorous necessity) we took our places in the diligence for Geneva. At 2 o'clock on a Sunday afternoon we mounted the Imperiale of the coach in the office of the Messageries Royales and proceeded on our journey. It was a roomy and not uncomfortable compartment – with a hood and a curtain against the wind and the rain, and not very hard cushions. I can't say the views were beautiful or the aspect of the road anything but tiresome. The only relief I felt was in ascending hills, when the whole company inside and outside, turned out for the luxury of a walk which mitigated the cramping annoyance of our long sitting.

The road was still and monotonous in the last degree. The stoppages were not frequent excepting only at the stages where changed, and the Inns (at which we did stop) were men and miserable. It had been announced in the programme that we should sleep at Dijon. We arrived at Dijon at about 9 at night. There we found a *table d'hôte* of very unsatisfactory appearance – but to such tired and hungry travelers as we were not unacceptable. Beds being mentioned, we were told they were ready, but we learned at the same time that the diligence would proceed at 2 o'clock in the morning. Such a prospect of a night's rest was by no means inviting so we determined not to avail ourselves of it – but chose to while away the time as well as we could. Neale relieved himself by turning our disappointment into verse – and I smoked a cigar. At 2 o'clock, i.e. in the dark night, we scrambled up to the Imperiale and in due time reached Lyons of which we only saw as much of the Place de Belle Cour and the grand edifices on the quai as could be commanded from the top of the coach.

We then soon began to ascend the Jura where every step brought before us views of the utmost beauty, variety and novelty. But the crowing delight we experienced was the scene that opened upon us after attaining the topmost ridge of the Jura and having passed the Fort de l'Écluse, this is so well known and has been so often described that I would not dwell upon it, even if I did not feel the impossibility of doing it justice. Although therefore I forbear from details, I cannot pass it by without chronicling it as one of the most beautiful and delightful sights I had then or have at any time beheld. The grand expanse – the matchless panorama – the spacious fertile plain – the glittering blue lake – the distant city of Geneva – and above all the stupendous Majesty and beauty of Mont Blanc were positively overwhelming and we could not find words to express our surprise and delight. The sun was declining and the "Rose hues" which it shed upon the grand mountain were irresistibly charming. We stood gazing at it as long as the tyrant conductor would permit us and then resuming our places – greatly enjoying every part of the scenery we traversed – and never losing sight of the "Monarch of Mountains" we proceeded and alighted at the Ecu de Genève at about 8 o'clock in the evening of the Thursday after our departure from Paris. (What changes railways have made for travelers!)

Two days we spent in Geneva, of which the greater part was passed upon the lake. "The blue rushing of the arrowy Rhone," as it hurried on and passes the city. I was in those days a swimmer and greatly delighted in the exercise. I went in the very early morning to indulge in a bath at a spot half a mile below the city at a place where I saw persons availing themselves of such accommodation as had been provided for the purpose. I enjoyed the rapid course of the water and was interested in the marked difference between the intense blue of the Rhone, and the milky colour of a stream which flowed into it – but when I thought of returning I found it impossible to swim against the current and was compelled to gain the bank but at a considerable distance from the spot at which I had deposited my clothes. Fortunately, there were no persons passing at so early an hour and I was able to get back without committing any offence against decency though not until after accomplishing a very toilsome walk over a very rough path.

We proceeded in a *char-à-banc* to Chamounix, made the usual ascent to the Mer de Glace, the Jardin, etc., and visited the source of the river (Arveyron) and saw the other wonders of the place and went thence, on foot, over the Col de Balme to Villebeuve. By the same mode of travelling, we reached Chillon and visited the dungeon from which Bonnivard "appealed from tyranny to God;" cast long looks and sighs over the rocks of Meillerie and the Bosquet de Julie – saw in the church at Vevey the tomb of John Kemble, who spent there the last days of his retirement from his theatrical triumphs – and after inspecting Vevey and the other places between the head of the lake and Lausanne and with much thought and talk of nothing but Voltaire and Rousseau and Gibbon and Byron and Madame de Staël, names inseparable from the places we passed – and found everything so pleasant and above all so new that no words can express the delight we experienced. From Lausanne, the laborious and tiresome diligence carried us back to Paris. By this time our resources were wholly exhausted. Neale, however, was enabled to borrow in Paris from a friend of his father's money enough to carry us home. I arrived in London somewhat ragged – very hungry and penniless, but with a store of recollections, which have furnished me with lasting pleasure and which have been probably not without profit in my subsequent career.

More Journalism

My restlessness and dissatisfaction with my condition were by no means appeased – but on the contrary much aggravated by my travels. I continued to scribble – and having become acquainted with some men connected to the press I sought to procure employment in that branch of industry. I had an interview with Mr. Perry then the somewhat famous editor *The Morning Chronicle* (the organ of the Whig party), who treated me with great civility – but whose establishment offered no vacancy. I had no better success with Mr. Thwaites, the proprietor – and was called editor of a newspaper called *The Morning Herald*. He was a retired linen-draper – very coarse and ignorant, but industrious and bent only on making as much money as he could out of his publication in which he was for some time successful. From him, I obtained some slight employment in the way of reports and theatrical and other criticisms – but all this seemed to lead to nothing. An evening newspaper was established by the Society of Commercial Travellers who purchased a failing paper called *The Globe*, and engrafted upon it a new one with the title of the *Globe and Traveller* with a view of retaining as much as they could of the old connection but with very sanguine hopes of making a profitable affair by means of their influence in the various country places which were visited by their numerous and active members.

The prospect was upon the first appearance of the paper encouraging. The management was in the hands of the most prominent of the members of the society, who formed a committee of directors. The editor was Mr. Quin, who was author of a book of travels chiefly in the Levant, as well as I recollect. Beyond a certain facility of scribbling upon any given subject his qualifications for the office he undertook were very inconsiderable. The staff of the paper was composed of Irishmen, most of whom had been employed upon other papers.

One of these was a gentleman was called Dr. Walsh. How he came by his title I never learned. He had been an army surgeon and had been through the Peninsular Campaign. He was about forty years old and was in a miserable state of health occasioned by habitual intemperance. He was by no means devoid of talent, had some learning, and was reputed to have taken in his youth a creditable degree at Trinity College, Dublin. His friends believed – for he had told them so – that he had written a tragedy by which he hoped and did not doubt that he should establish a reputation far beyond that of any modern poet. He talked of this work, which was all but finished with great confidence, but with some moderation in his sober moments but when, as was too frequently the case, whisky punch had obtained the command of his soul, he did not scruple to proclaim himself as the only indisputable successor of Shakespeare. He had been appointed the sub-editor of the *Globe and Traveller* – and labored very diligently in that calling. A part of his duty consisted in selecting and abridging from other papers domestic and foreign such articles of intelligence as suited the passing day. With a serviceable pair of scissors and a paste pot he supplied the columns of the *Globe and Traveller* with abundant and valuable news and occasionally added to them his own original observations. But a difficulty occurred which he had not contemplated upon assuming his office. Although he had passed some years abroad in Spain – and for some time in France, – he had neglected his opportunity of becoming acquainted with foreign languages – and now consequently found himself greatly embarrassed in rendering into English the extracts he had to make from the French and Italian and other papers. I had become in some degree acquainted with him and he confided to me the trouble and doubt which he experienced – and had occasionally applied to me to help him. He was a good-natured person and his conversation in his sober moments (the praises he bestowed upon his embryo tragedy apart) amusing and even instructive. I very readily assisted him – but as the occasions when he required help became more frequent and urgent – the French newspapers requiring at that time constant care and caution, he proposed that I should undertake the selection and translation of the French and Italian extracts (the others were not considered important) and should for that purpose take a seat at his sub-editorial table. For this he offered me a guinea and a half a week – his own salary being five guineas, and I not unwillingly accepted these terms. He was at this time enjoying his military pension, which with the reduced amount of his salary left him a sufficient income for his very simple style of living and for indulgence in his favorite beverage, so that I had no scruple in engaging with him.

The scissors and the pastepot were transferred to me, and for several months I not only did the work I had agreed for but a good deal more. For the poor doctor's ailments were greatly increased. His asthma, which alcohol did not improve, overcame him, and after being confined to his bed for some time he died – and I don't think his other tragedy was otherwise completed. The proprietors of the paper then offered me the post which had thus become vacant – but as the success of the paper had become more doubtful than they had anticipated, they intimated to me that they could not afford to pay more than three guineas a week. I was of course very sorry that the public were so regardless of the merit of such labours as I had bestowed for their edification – and still more sorry that the salary was to be reduced. At the same time, I must confess I was glad enough to get it – and so I became *en titre* the sub-editor of the *Globe and Traveller*.

The duties of my new post were not very heavy – but they required constant and punctual application. I had not altogether relinquished the business of the attorney's office, although it had become much less considerable than formerly. My editorship required me to be at work from an early hour in the morning – not later than eight o'clock, when the letters and foreign papers came by post – and continued til one o'clock when the paper went to press – so I had to make a rapid run from Clerkenwell to Shoe Lane, sometimes in bad weather and always through a very nasty route by Saffron Hill and Field Lane (then most horrible expanses – now clean and commodious streets). However, with such strength and spirits as I then possessed I got through all this without murmur – and not without thanks for my good luck. Too good, alas, to last. The newspaper was declining and after about three months the governing body determined not to continue their losing game. They gave a fortnight's notice to each of the members of their staff and when that period expired my office came to an end and my salary ceased. I must confess that my disappointment was great at that time but I was not dejected. My hopes were bright, and after a few weeks I found myself much better off than if my editorship had been continued. I had contracted an acquaintance with several newspaper men and was known in several quarters as a candidate for an engagement whenever a vacancy should occur.

The London Times and Gray's Inn

There happened at this time a *cause célébre* which excited great public interest. A man named Weare had been murdered at Elstree by a notorious ruffian named Thurtell, and some of his comrades, under circumstances of treachery and cruelty which distinguished the strong suspicions which were entertained it appeared to be doubtful whether the guilt could be brought home to the persons accused. They were put upon their trial at Hertford – and unless my memory fails me, they were tried by a special commission. The corps of reporters for the *Times* was so much employed about other matters as to require some assistance. I received a note from Mr. Barnes, with whom I had an interview when he offered me the job of reporting this trial – at the same time guarding himself against its being understood as more than a merely temporary engagement. I very readily undertook it and went to Hertford. The trial lasted several days and was in all respects very important and interesting. I did my work as well as I could, and I believe to the satisfaction of my employers. Mr. Barnes thanked me very graciously – I was liberally paid and in less than a month afterward I obtained a regular engagement on the *Times* at 5 guineas a week.

I considered this then – and as I now consider it – a turning point in my destiny. I was relieved from the hazards and uncertainty which had frequently caused me anxiety. I had a fixed regular employment, the duties of which imposed upon me responsibilities of weight – and ensured my steadiness. I had formed a strong regard for Hugh Evans, the Doctor's second son – and our friendship became most intimate. He had now just finished the term of his articles with Mr. William Bromley of Gray's Inn – and was about to set up for himself as an attorney. For this purpose, he had taken chambers on the second floor of No. 2 Gray's Inn Square. They were commodious and in all respects convenient and agreeable – and being much more spacious than he required he proposed that we should share them. I became the occupant of a very pleasant room looking over the Gardens, admirably suited for my pursuits – and wholly from any interruption from H's business and his clerk and clients. For clients he had from the beginning. He was so well known and so much liked by his father's numerous friends that he soon got into some employment – not, of course, extensive at first, but presenting a fair prospect of future success. His good looks, good temper and most obliging disposition made him a universal favorite. His high spirits and sanguine temper unfortunately led him into habits which were in the result very disastrous – but which I will not at present anticipate.

My father, who was very desirous that I should adopt some more stable pursuit than I was then engaged in, had looked about with that view and had spared no pains or care in endeavouring to find some suitable employment for me. He was upon friendly and intimate terms with many members of the profession – and among others with Sir George – then Mr. Rose, who was an equity draftsman in very good practice as a junior in the Court of Chancery and with a high reputation in the Bankruptcy department – which at that time was in few hands and rather lucrative. The system then prevailing was very different from that which has been since established after many changes – not of law so much as in the practice. The fees derived from it formed a considerable part of the Lord Chancellor's income and whatever complaints were made of the "Laws delay" in the Court of Chancery proper – it could not be denied that Lord Eldon attended very sedulously to the bankruptcy administration over which he presided not only as appellate judge – but as the sole authority regulating the issue of Commissions and controlling all the proceedings relating to their execution. He had besides the right of appointing commissioners in town and country – offices well worth the while of expectant junior barristers and often bestowed (it was said) more under the influence of personal and political motives than on account of the merits of those who were so fortunate as to engage the Chancellor's favourable notice. In one of his conversations with Mr. Rose (of which I must have been the subject) he, adopting I suppose, my father's too favourable opinion of my abilities, suggested to him that it would be worthwhile for me to be called to the bar – pointing out to him that although success might and must be precarious, yet there were many occasional opportunities in the lower grades in which some employment might be obtained while I could, in the meantime, pursue the avocations in which I was engaged. When this was first suggested to me, I was rather startled. I was not conceited enough to assure myself that such talents as I possessed would lead to success in the ambitious career which was thus presented to me. I had many long and serious conversations with my father who entertained the project favourably. He told me he did not think that I was qualified to shine as an attorney while under any circumstances a long time must elapse before I could count upon making any considerable income – and I should be obliged to devote all my time to the drudgery of the practice – while on the other hand I should be free to do what I could in the way of scribbling, and open to avail myself of any favourable chance that might occur – and vision of colonial judicial appointments and other employment for which a wig and gown were qualifications danced before our eyes.

"Being called to the bar was in those days the easiest and simplest thing in the world," my father was a Member of the Middle Temple – and had more than once thought of being called to the bar – but various circumstances – his family of ten children – his increasing years – but most of all the *res angusta domi* had prevented him from indulging in the pleasing dreams by which he was invited to that behemoth, although I am convinced that if he could have commanded the requisite qualification he would certainly have attained distinction. He had all the qualities which ensure success, superior natural talents, accurate and profound knowledge of the law of real property – a knowledge which recent changes have dispensed with, but which then was held in high esteem – perhaps the higher because it was possessed by only a small number of the practitioners, a high and honorable spirit and industry indefatigable. But there was an impediment by my adopting Mr. Rose's advice which seemed to us to be insurmountable. In order to be called to the Bar it was not only necessary to keep terms, i.e., to dine on certain days of each term during 5 years – but to deposit a sum of £100 of caution money with the steward. As, however, it was not necessary that this deposit would be made immediately upon my becoming a member of the Inn, it was determined that I should be entered at least – and I was accordingly so entered, trusting to the future to provide for the deposit. At the end of two years, Hugh Evans got from his father a cheque for the LBB100 – and I continued to keep my terms in the Hall at Gray's Inn with due regularity until the five years were accomplished and I was call to the bar.

Upon taking up my residence in Gray's Inn, I wholly relinquished my connection with the solicitor's office and was free to devote myself to my new occupation, the most urgent and serious of which was reporting the speeches in Parliament for the *Times*. This work was not altogether new but was rather arduous. I had a very slight knowledge of the art of shorthand writing – but with a very good memory and under a sense of the importance of my task and with the kind assistance of the older hands in the gallery I soon found myself able to take such notes of the debates as enabled me to transcribe a fair report and to the satisfaction of the editor.

While Parliament was sitting this work was hard – occasionally very hard. The *Times* had a numerous staff of reporters who succeeded each other in taking notes. From a quarter of an hour to twenty minutes was the duration of each turn – and the notes then taken furnished materials which it usually took two hours to transcribe for the compositors. The walk from the House of Commons to Printing House Square could not be performed in less than three quarters of an hour – and this had to be performed in all weathers – often long after midnight and upon some extraordinary occasions it was necessary to repeat the process. Tired no doubt I sometimes was – but in those days I did not think that bodily fatigue was any cause for complaint. My copy finished and in the hands of the printer I trudged to my quarters in Gray's Inn – always very late at night, or early before the sun was up. My latchkey was my passport – the tinder box on the mantlepiece was familiarly accessible – and I tumbled into bed satisfied that I should see the result of my labours in the morning paper. While Parliament was sitting my work was almost exclusively confined to the gallery and the printing office. During the other months of the year, I was employed in reporting cases in the Courts of Law – but principally in the Equity Courts – an arrangement that suited admirably the schemes I had begun to form as to my future progress and during the summer Assizes I reported the law cases on the Midland and Home Circuits. Occasionally, I was entrusted with theatrical criticisms and descriptions of exhibitions of paintings and other spectacles, and sometimes had the task of condensing the contents of Blue Books – and of pronouncing upon the merits of literary novelties. A liberal holiday of three or four weeks in the dullest part of the year of which I availed myself by making trips across the Channel in which I revisited Paris and took flying glances at Belgium and Holland.

We had very soon established a very comfortable home in our chambers – our acquaintances became numerous. H. E. was very fond of society and his knack of making friends was irresistible, while I also was not unwilling to collect friends about us. Our evenings when the House was not sitting were often very pleasant. On grand occasions we got very good, but not very costly dinners sent in hot from the Gray's Inn Coffee House where were on the best terms with the head waiter and manager. At other times our clever old laundress would get us a leg or a shoulder of mutton dressed at the baker's – which served us cold for a day and sometimes two days afterwards – and this was occasionally enlivened by a wild duck dressed in the same manner and supplied by a fat old rogue of a poulterer in Lamb's Conduit Street, who affected to take great interest in us and our repasts. The suppers were divine. Mrs. Bettridge in Homer Court was an admirable artist in oysters of all sorts – crabs stewed – roasted with crumbs – or in their native beauty and simplicity; and such lobster and crabs as I had never seen before and have never since seen surpassed. Hugh E., who was very fond of everything theatrical (our earliest acquaintance began behind the scenes at Sadler's Wells), had formed an intimacy with the renowned Arthur Bunn, the manager of both the theatres royal. Billy Dunn, the treasurer at Drury Lane, was an old friend of mine. Yates, the father of the present famous editor and novelist – Russell the Jerry Sneak then a very old man – Munden and several others of the same class whose names I cannot at this moment pause to recollect joined in the revels which were always prolonged into the smaller hours after midnight. I cannot say that this was very wise – but I know it was very pleasant and was neither injurious to health or morals. Gin and water, our chief drink, was not extravagant, and I have not to regret that any culpable excesses stained our merriment – though I don't deny that our time might have been better employed.

We had occasionally visitors of graver character and who kept better hours. Ned Prentis, then a pupil of Haydon's, Edwin Landseer and his brother Charles, and his other brother Tom, who became a famous engraver, were several times our guests with some other Tapins, students in art – all of whom obtained more or less renown, though at the time I speak of they were merely feeling their way in their careers. They were, one and all, very simple honest fellows and their society was most pleasant. There were some older fellows who had already begun to establish reputations, Creswick, Stanfield, Roberts, Linton, Cartwright – a retired naval officer who had adopted marine painting as a profession, and who died before he had displayed remarkable skill which was greatly enhanced by his nautical knowledge. In Gray's Inn and in their own quarters we found these painters very agreeable associates.

Besides these we received older and more serious visitors. Prentis had carried me to see Godwin, then a very old man keeping (nominally) a bookseller's shop in Pickett Street, St. Clements. The author of Caleb Williams and many other works had enjoyed such notoriety that I was very desirous of becoming acquainted with him. I accordingly readily availed myself of P's introduction – and was greatly interested in the conversation of this remarkable man notwithstanding the terror which his name had inspired by childish years. His years and infirmities had quenched his vivacity – but he was good tempered – full of knowledge – very ready to talk and always talking to the purpose upon literary subjects in which I naturally took great interest.

He accepted my invitation to drink tea in Grays' Inn. His wife and his friend Charles Lamb (Elia) and Miss Lamb were of the party at which I first saw him. On his agreeing to come to tea, I extended my invitation to the other persons present, which they very graciously accepted – and accordingly a few days afterwards they ascended our stairs. I had prepared a regale of tea and coffee, Sally Lunns and cake. They seemed pleased and I believe found themselves comfortable. After tea we turned to whist, of which they were all very fond. The conversation was cheerful and occasionally merry. Mrs. Godwin was unquestionably a clever woman who had seen a good deal of the world and was not unwilling to enjoy all that remained of it. Charles Lamb – an old looking, pinched-up little man – dressed in black with knee breeches and woolen stockings of the same colour and linen not of the most brilliant whiteness. Poor Miss Lamb (the subject of that most dreadful tragedy which has been so often told) was a fat old lady muffled up in black bombazine – generally silent – but not looking sad – and playing her rubber with alacrity. I cannot recollect any particular witticism or drollery on the part of C. Lamb – but he was very cheerful and agreeable and appeared to like his entertainment – for he promised to come again – and the whole party kept the promise.

At Godwin's I met Mrs. Shelley, who had come soon after her husband's death to England with her little boy – the present Sir Percy Shelley. [He died in March 1890]. She was not upon good terms with her husband's father Sir Timothy Shelley, who desired to have possession of the boy to which, of course, she would not consent. She was very scantily (if at all) provided for, and preferred to live by her own exertions to accepting what the baronet offered upon <u>his</u> conditions. By contributions to magazines and other casual literary labours, she contrived to maintain her independence – until the old man was induced to give in – and a satisfactory arrangement was come to by which the suitable education of the child was secured and a fit provision for the mother was made without any sacrifice of her feelings. I met her very frequently about this time – and I must say that I conceived great respect for her character and the patience with which she bore her great affliction. Under other circumstances than those which befell her she would have been distinguish not only for her intellectual power – but for great goodness and all estimable feminine qualities. Upon the reconciliation – or whatever it ought to be called with the baronet – she quitted London and died not long afterwards. I believe her latter days were passed in perfect comfort and tranquility.

If I had more time to bestow upon the task I have set myself I could set down some remembrances of the gentlemen of the press whom I became unavoidably acquainted at this period. John Payne Collier, an experienced shorthand writer, much valued at the *Times* for his industry and dispatch who upon his retirement with a pension and the savings he had made, employed himself in researches connected with the literary history of writers in and about the age of Queen Elizabeth and the persons connected with the stage of that day and published many works full of earnest industry but not distinguished by much judgment or any taste. Tyas, who had established a brilliant reputation at Cambridge – where he was resident with Barnes, but who on coming to London found no such encouragement as he had expected and satisfied his ambition by becoming a reporter. Rheumatism and a fondness for strong drink made his latter days cloudy. John Henry Barrow, a lively, clever fellow full of good spirits, – but frivolous and without the ballast of principle. He afterwards deserted from the *Times* and joined the *Daily News* – travelled for the latter to India and many other foreign parts but without any good fortune. His sister was the mother of Charles Dickens.

There were besides many Irishmen – all active, ready witted, but all of them improvident. Jemmy Woods and his brother Roger, David Power who had in his intractable imprudence forfeited a very good colonial appointment, Michael Nugen, O'Reilly, James and Tom Haynes, Ned Byrne, and Peter Finnerly, an old and famous rebel who had come under the clutches of the law and had suffered the martyrdom of imprisonment in Ireland. He was now past labour but lived upon the renown he had established. And there were several others – all of them disappointed men who had seen better days and who found in the press a refuge in which they could at least live. How much they had to complain of against Fortune – or how much ought to be set down to errors of their own it is not possible to guess. They are all departed – long ago – so there can be no great harm in saying that they were much given to drink and much in debt at all times. They were, however, good-natured and almost always in good spirits. A more cheerful place than the sanded parlour the back of the Cart and Horses, a public house in St. Martin's Lane opposite Aldridge's Repository, I don't think could be found in all London. In the daytime this place was resorted to by the dealers in horses of all kinds – but after nine o'clock at night and thenceforward to near midnight it is wholly consecrated to the more intellectual persons I have been mentioning. Not that it was confined to them. Thither came some of the tradesmen in the neighborhood, attracted no doubt by the charms of the conversation which was always there going on and most of them connected in some degree with the fine arts. Some picture dealers – a picture frame maker – a mezzo-tint engraver – one Meyer who regretted that the peace (after Waterloo) had destroyed his trade which had been flourishing while he was fully employed in engraving the portraits of the "Heroes who bled for their Country" but was now confined to casual lords mayor and a few members of Parliament. Several painters, some actors, joined occasionally. The conversation was generally amusing. With the exception of Mr. Macguire, a leather breeches maker who had a shop next door but one in the lane – and who was the only silent Irishman I ever knew – and whom I have sometimes since thought may have been in the employment of the police – most of the guests had something to say upon matters in which all were more or less interested. All were civil and cheerful – I never saw or heard of any excess or interruption of the harmony which prevailed. I have been in many societies more refined and intellectual but none in which a man who was tired could repose himself for an hour or two more satisfactorily.

My visits to the Cart and Horses were not very frequent, however agreeable – nor was much of the leisure I had while I dwelt in Gray's Inn at all dissipated. The prospect of being called to the bar was always before me and I did the best I could with such opportunity as I had to qualify myself for what I had determined would be my future. And I cannot say that I was not fortunate in such opportunities. Hon Evans – Hugh's older brother – had been called to the bar and had set up in chambers as an equity draftsman and conveyancer. He had spent a year in the chambers of Bellenden Kerr, a conveyancer of repute – and six months with an equity pleader whose name I do not remember. John Evans gave me free access to his chambers and his papers – advised me what to read and how to read and explained to me the mysteries into which I was to be initiated. My brother Henry had also begun to practice as a conveyancer and his clear head and most affectionate heart were bestowed upon me in my pursuit with indefatigable solicitude. I had no money to pay the usual fees to tutors – but I possessed two tutors better and more efficient than money could buy. I read with as much diligence and earnestness as I could command the elementary books which were requisite, and the Reports in Chancery from [William] Peere Williams to [Francis] Vesey.

During this time, I was employed sometimes in scribbling of various kinds – and I had obtained admission to the Reading Room of the British Museum. To this invaluable treasury, I very frequently resorted in the daytime, and I owe it a most deep debt of gratitude. By the assistance which I there obtained I was enabled not unfrequently to discharge the duties other than reporting, which the *Times* occasionally cast upon me and, unless I am mistaken, establish a character in that establishment somewhat above the ordinary run of several of my colleagues.

Laura Again

In all these desultory pursuits there was one fixed and bright spot to which my whole thoughts were directed – and which occupied my whole soul – and formed the motive of all my exertions, – the guiding star of my existence! I had conceived the warmest, purest love for that dear being whom I afterwards called my own – and had the supreme happiness of knowing that my affection was returned. I cannot write upon this subject. We had talked of our hopes and prospects which were by no means cheerful at times, but which were sustained by mutual confidence and by that true good sense and courage on her part which enabled us to overcome difficulty seemingly unsurmountable. The embarrassments into which her father had fallen had grown to an alarming extent – and he was compelled to give up his establishment and to withdraw from England with such remnant of his fortunes as he could manage to keep together. His family consisted of his wife, three daughters and one son – and it was ultimately determined that they should go together to Belgium. This state of things put an end to the doubts which had so long disturbed and disheartened us. I had the prospect of securing (if such an expression could be applied to my condition) an income small enough no doubt – but which after long and mature discussion we determined should be made enough for the hazardous experiment we resolved to try. I proposed that my dearest Laura should not form one of the fugitive family – but that she should be entrusted to me.

It would be idle to dwell upon the difficulties which were raised. Mr. and Mrs. Cook had hoped that their daughter would have made a much more satisfactory marriage than I could offer – and probably would have rejected my proposition without hesitation – but our united prayers and such pressure as the circumstances exercised at length prevailed, and on the 23rd April 1827 we were married in Enfield Church. After passing the rest of the day at Clay Hill, my wife and I returned to Corton Street where I had taken a house which we had furnished partly with contributions from Woodbridge House, partly with purchases out of the very moderate means we possessed – and by long and by large, I hardly know how – my dear wife managed to make us a most happy home which we occupied for the ensuing seven years.

(Mem. An episode which must not interrupt the narrative: In August 1887 I had written thus far – the principal part while I was staying with dear Sis at Sudbury. I then went with Aunt Fanny and Frank to Compton – where after a fortnight, or so, we were joined by Lydia and Nelly, and Susan and Jem. They left us after a short stay – the two younger ones to their several schools and the others to join their father and mother in a foreign trip to Meran, Bozen, etc., and we saw no more of them till the middle of November, when they came back having enjoyed their excursion – all in good health and spirits. We stayed on at Compton enjoying greatly the unexampled fine weather and perfect repose, interrupted only by Frank's lawn-tennis parties, until, early in October, Frank's judicial duties called him to London – and here we have remained. Besides some not very serious indisposition, I have found myself assailed by a long fit of indolence which I try to overcome with very indifferent success – I have however so much to be thankful for that it would be most unreasonable to complain of what, after all, "'is merely' the sickness of long life – old age" – and as it is not my wish or intention to make this a chronicle of lamentation I will even take up my story in this month of December 1887.)

Marriage and First Legal Practice

My life after my marriage underwent a change – new views, different habits, thoughts which I had not before entertained occupied me. I took chambers in Field Court, Gray's Inn, and settled myself to such work as I might find. Little enough, in the way of my profession, that was for some months. I engaged a clerk, which was a necessary part of the establishment at least to open the door when and if anyone should knock – and to keep guard upon the quarters in my absence. And in this I was very fortunate – a boy of about 14 years old who had just left his school, and could read and write very well, presented himself and he became my slave for seven shillings a week with a prospect of advancement if all should go well. From the spring of 1827 to the close of 1886, he was my faithful and most valuable assistant. I may have more to say of him hereafter, for the present I am bound to express my opinion that I have never ceased to think of him as an upright able honourable man.

I was very frequently absent from Chambers. The mornings were generally occupied in attending the Courts of Equity – one of which was then occasionally held in the old Court of Exchequer (in term time at Westminster) and at the other sittings at Lincoln's Inn, the Rolls, or such other place as the Exchequer might find refuge. The evenings I almost always passed at home, (not without occupation of some kind) when I had not to attend the gallery of the House of Commons – and there occasionally the debates were sometimes so long that I could not get to bed until long after the next day had begun to shine. The hardest part of this was that my dear wife could not be prevailed upon to go to bed until my return. The work was sometimes hard – but in those days health and good spirits enabled me to get through it without difficulty and the sweet co-operation of my dearest lightened my labours and threw a perpetual sunshine on my path.

In those days it was the almost general custom for the younger members of the Chancery Bar to attend Quarter Sessions. Many of them had local connections, and all of them knew or had been told that Quarter Sessions formed a good school for beginners – as it undoubtedly did and many examples were pointed out of illustrious advocates who had learned the use of their weapons in that school, and who had found that the Sessions was a path which led to the highest distinctions. Sir Samuel Romilly, Sir Charles Wetherell and many other advocates of the utmost eminence had practiced there. At the very time of which I am now writing, Mr. [Robert] Rolfe was a conveyancer and equity draftsman in Lincoln's – he had attended not only Sessions but had obtained the lead of the Norfolk Circuit which he only relinquished when and because his practice in equity had greatly increased. And this to such an extent that he remained at the bar until he was made a Vice-Chancellor [and twice served as Lord Chancellor].

With the inducement which such a prospect presented I boldly determined that I would go to Sessions, and although I determined that I would continue to try my fortune in the Court of Chancery, I resolved also to join a circuit so that I might at least not be disqualified if any favorable chance might offer itself.

I therefore became a Member of the Home Circuit and joined the Surrey Sessions Bar – and this for several good reasons. The distances from London were less than any others by which the expenditure of both time and money were diminished. The Sessions had besides this advantage, that, in addition to the quarterly meetings, an adjourned Sessions was held every six weeks at Horsemonger Lane which I could easily reach on foot – while the jealous etiquette of the bar of that day prohibited barristers from travelling in the public conveyance, a ridiculous rule which we supposed to be founded upon the notion that they might be prejudiced, and their forensic virtue might be imperiled by communication with parties and witnesses with whom they might afterwards have to deal with in court.

I went several times to the Assize towns Hertford, Chelmsford, Lewes, Maidstone, and Guildford, without any encouragement other than a very few stray junior briefs which I got because there happened to be no one else to hold them – and I held several like unimportant briefs for happier men who were engaged in another court. Upon the whole the circuit expenses were a good deal more than any pecuniary gain I got, but I saw and earned experience which I believe did help me much.

I had one *cause célèbre* which I ought not to forget. At the Croydon Assizes, before Mr. Justice Gaselee, a very miserable, poor, old woman was arraigned for the murder of another poor old woman of unsound mind who had been for some years entrusted to the prisoner's care. An inquest had been held where the master of the workhouse and the parish beadle and the parish doctor had given evidence to the general effect that the prisoner had treated her ward cruelly, and that her body exhibited marks of bruises said to have been caused by blows from a stick used by the prisoner for intimidating and restraining her sometimes refractory ward. Upon this evidence the jury had returned a verdict of willful murder – and the parish prosecuting, the scared and half imbecile old creature (she was between 70 and 80 years of age) was placed at the bar to be tried for her life. Scared and bewildered she, with the help of the gaoler, pleaded not guilty. No one appeared for her – she had apparently no friends. The judge said the charge was serous, and she ought to have counsel and he called upon me as a junior to look after the case on her behalf. Of course I could not refuse – but as it was somewhat late in the afternoon of Saturday the judge said he would not proceed with the case til the following Monday – and he directed that the deposition should in the meantime be handed to me that I might see the nature of the case made before the coroner's jury. I was heartily glad of this respite and went home pondering very deeply upon the fate which had befallen me – and not a little embarrassed as to how I should acquit myself of a task so awful and so new to me.

At this time counsel were not allowed to address the jury on behalf of the prisoner. They might call witnesses for the defense and were permitted to cross examine those for the prosecution. I had no witnesses to call, my only chance therefore lay in the cross examination. The doctor's appeared to me to be the only formidable testimony in which, however, I thought I perceived a trace of hesitation that might yield upon pressure. Some of the terms of art which he had employed puzzled me and, in order to get a clearer notion upon that most material part of the case, I betook myself to an intimate friend of mine, William Lyon, a young surgeon then beginning to practice. We read the doctor's deposition –

considered it very carefully. I treasured up all that Lyon told me about bedsore and ecchymosis, and appearances after death, and other matters which greatly enlarged my knowledge and, in the result, felt myself able to cross examine the doctor without making my poor client's case worse than it had been left – bad as that appeared to be.

On Monday, of course, I was at Croydon. The doctor, who I believe was an honest man enough, admitted that he had never seen the old woman in her life – but still adhered to his opinion that the bruises and their consequences were sufficient to have caused her death – and as he could find no other cause he repeated his opinion. I had sense enough to forbear pressing him on this, but I managed to persuade him to confess that he had no experience and very little knowledge of the effects which might be produced by ecchymosis (a capital hard word of which neither judge nor jury knew the meaning) before or after death. In short, after a very favorable summing up by the good-natured merciful old judge, the jury acquitted the Prisoner. Thus ended my "great first (criminal) cause." Everybody was satisfied and I confess I was greatly pleased.

The Surrey Sessions, besides being very useful to me in my progress, was very pleasant. The bar was composed of agreeable men. Barnewell, the editor of many volumes of Common Law Reports, was in name and standing the Leader – but Thesiger had by far the largest portion of the business. Barnewell was many years the senior – and a most gentleman-like person, well informed and well bred, of an old English Roman Catholic family, and held in well-deserved esteem in Westminster Hall but deficient in the qualities which most find favor with the attorneys. Thesiger, active, clever, shallow, but most thoroughly painstaking: very fond of joking – of ready wit, which though not of the most brilliant kind was full of mirth and good nature. There was a somewhat solemn old gentleman Mr. Cowley, often his opponent and sometimes his butt, who had a good share of the business, but was chiefly renowned as the son of a lady who in her time had enjoyed some literary reputation and was authoress of a successful comedy (*The Belle's Stratagem*). Jemmett, the son of a Kingston attorney and brother of the then existing coroner, was in very good practice. Ross, the West Indian, and one of the four principal counsel of the Marshalsea – or Palace Court, Charles Maclean, son of a

Scotch lord, was backed by influence of some kind but I forget what it was – and dear Montagu Chambers, always full of fun and of inexhaustible good spirits and good nature. Besides these there were several others, all juniors, and all pleasant companions. To me and to them briefs were merely accidental and very few. But I must not forget my first brief at Sessions. There existed then a rule (by what authority it was established I know not) – but it was rule – that no counsel not belonging to the Surrey Sessions could appear unless he was associated with a Member of the Sessions as his junior. Johnny Willcock, who had been recently called to the bar, had, by way of distinguishing himself published a small legal tract "On the Duties of a Parish Constable" a work that enjoyed some popularity, at least among licensed victualers and was, no doubt, valuable in its way. A constable had been fined by magistrates in petty sessions for some dereliction of duty and being dissatisfied with the decision had appealed to the Quarter Sessions – and had retained Willcock, who appeared as his counsel.

On the attorney being informed by Mr. Lawson, the Clerk of the Peace, of the existence of the Rule – a form of a brief was prepared on the instant and delivered to the *Juvenissimus* of the bar. I happened to be the one so favored by fortune and received the guinea and followed the argument of my leader, which as well as I recollect turned on the construction of an Act of Parliament. I cannot permit myself to doubt that we were quite right; but I can't deny that our appeal was dismissed. However, I got my first guinea at Sessions and, what was better, made the acquaintance of one of the best natured men (Willcock) I ever knew, though as O'Donovan said of him after bearing testimony to Johnny's sterling qualities, "I must confess, Sir, that his manner is not attractive." (Note: Poor O'Donovan through some Irish influence got appointed Attorney General at one of the West Indies Islands – but was so ill on the voyage that he never assumed the office – and came home. In recounting his sufferings to Thesiger he described in great detail the horrors he had endured. "For many days, Sir" he said "I could not keep anything on my stomach – I threw up everything." "And the worst of all," said Thesiger with true compassion "was that you threw up your place.")

Upon the whole the Sessions – and especially the country part of it – was agreeable though by no means lucrative. The expenses of lodgings and traveling were the most formidable of its features, and although I kept them within the narrowest bounds they told somewhat upon my small income. I shared the lodgings with Jemmett – I did not always dine at the mess – I did always dine with such of the magistrates who were so good as to invite the bar – and with the Clerk of the Peace Lawson, a man well-to-do and who was generous and hospitable and particularly encouraging to juniors. When the Session was held at Kingston, it was within a walk – barely ten miles which I have several times managed with great satisfaction and without more fatigue than in those days I could easily bear.

On one occasion Chambers, who was a good walker, and I had agreed upon the march. At that time, an opposition in the coaching interest had sprung up – and one of the competing establishments advertised that it had determined to abolish the practice of giving tips to the coachmen and guards – a custom universal, and universally grumbled at. As we strode over Wimbledon Common, and all along we found exhibited large and conspicuous placards "Cheap Travelling and No Fees" – Ominous and prophetic. Cheap our travelling was – and true enough it was that upon that turn neither of us got any fees. We had a good healthy walk – and the recollection furnished both of us a hearty laugh at the Bencher's table in Lincoln's Inn in later years when matters had a good deal changed with both of us.

By degrees, however, the adjoined Sessions in Horsemonger Lane, southward, became a little more profitable. In the country the best of the business consisted of appeals from petty sessions in pauper settlement cases. They were worth the while of the attorneys in the shape of costs – and the briefs went as a matter of course to the leaders. In Southwark almost all the cases were small misdemeanours, larcenies (petit), assaults and such like, beneath the attention of highly respectable attorneys and not yielding fees large enough to tempt the leaders of the bar. In this state of things, there grew up a small crop of irregular practitioners to whose management the conduct of the case was committed. Mr. Chester, a tall venerable-looking man was the most eminent of these – and was a well conducted man. He was said to have been butler to a former judge. He had picked up a small knowledge of Sessions law – and was said by Charles Law (one of Lord Ellenborough's sons, afterwards Recorder of London) to be one of the most respectable members of the profession for he always wore a clean shirt and paid the clerk's fee as well as the barristers. There was a Jew named Isaacs, generally considered a thief's attorney. He wore powder (then long out of fashion); he never had a clean shirt – but he wore in his front frill a diamond brooch worth money enough to buy the judge and jury and the bar. He resigned but a short time after I became acquainted with the court – but while he stayed he was regarded as a first-rate man in his line at the Old Bailey and elsewhere. There were two or three others who practiced rather irregularly – were not always punctual in paying the fees – and not infrequently in liquor. By long and by large however I did get a few guineas, some experience and, what was more substantially valuable, I got to be somewhat known by name.

Courts of Chancery and More Writing

Business in the Court of Chancery came very slowly. How it came at all I never could make out – for I had very few acquaintances among the attorneys and such of them as I did know were not often engaged in Chancery cases – and when they were they naturally preferred older hands for their work. I was, however, always sufficiently employed. I did a good deal of scribbling and although I look with anything but pride upon my literary labours I am very sensible of and grateful for he pecuniary assistance I derived from them. I undertook a life of Francis I [of France] for Edward Bull of Holles Street – and completed two volumes – not without a good deal of very hard work – for which I received £220. I wrote 2 volumes of tales for Robins for which he gave me £50. I edited a Pocket Magazine for him, and contributed largely to Lett's *European Magazine*, wrote weekly a leading article for the *Stockport Gazette*, a country newspaper which, however, did not live more than about a year. Some parts of that time I received a guinea for each letter – but towards the end of the paper's existence the funds were exhausted (*ou il n'y a rien le Roi perd ses droits*) so I made a bad debt of about the last score of my contributions. I wrote a great many other things for newspapers and magazines – much more than I can accurately recollect, or that are worth trying to recollect. I was generally paid but not largely. The best of these accidental jobs consisted of biographical notices of some of the personages in *Lodges Portraits*. The work had been got up very lavishly by Harding the Bookseller (Harding, Lepard and Co., Pall Mall East), who had spent a great deal of time and money in collecting the portraits, getting them made and engraved by very good artists, and with the help of Lodge's name (he being of repute as an antiquary – and Honorary King at Arms to boot) had established a very successful sale. The work was approaching completion when Lodge, who was an old man, found his energies failing and wanted assistance. Harding, who was, of course, much interested in bringing his work to a conclusion proposed the task to me. I wrote first a memoir of Lord Bolingbroke which was submitted to Lodge, who was pleased to approve of and praise it. I wrote several others, all of which were adopted. Harding paid like a prince, ten guineas for each of them. This was by far the most lucrative of all my scribbling exertions and brought me the acquaintance of Lodge, who was a very agreeable old gentleman, and of Harding, who was an admirable man of business – upright, clever and generous. He lived only a short time after the completion of his work, which was, however, so successful as to form a considerable part of the comfortable fortune he had realized.

None of these occupations however interfered with my persistent attendance upon the Court of Chancery. While it was sitting, I was there, always at hand – and before breakfast and after dinner – and sometimes late in the night I found time for my other labours.

I had been for some months in the occupation of my chambers in Field Court without seeing the ghost of a Chancery client when I received a visit from an old soldier whose name I forget. With some apologies for asking me to do what he required, he informed me that his usual draftsman (the old Roupell – then in first-rate practice) had drawn him a bill – but had been compelled suddenly to go out of town without completing the interrogating part of the draft, and this he asked me to supply – and, as time was pressing, with all possible dispatch. I consented and by the next morning the thing was done. The old gentleman was pleased and he said Roupell had told him he might supply the deficiency and although he believed he could, he preferred having more regular assistance partly because of the axiom *quiquis sui peritus*, which he quoted, but more because he believed that the defendant would be so much alarmed at the sight of long and searching interrogatories that he would succumb or at least compromise. He gave me two guineas, and, as he told me afterwards his expectations were realized, and he settle the suit to the satisfaction of his client. I never saw him again.

My first real patron – and my fast friend thenceforward – was Wetherall (Hard and Johnson). He was the Chancery manager of one of the largest London agency offices. How he found me out I never knew – but after trying me with some small matters he became a regular client and recommended me to many others. My chambers were hardly ever without some of his papers. He never marked large fees – but always fair and large enough and paid most punctually. I found the crossing to Lincoln's Inn from Holborn troublesome; so I transferred myself to Lincoln's Inn, became a Member of that Society – took Chambers in Old Square (No.22) and there established myself as a regular equity draftsman. I had no reason to regret the change. I believe that I had got the reputation (probably through Wetherell) of an expeditious workman, and was always to be found – the work at Sessions not causing any serious interruption.

I now found myself in a new atmosphere. My position was gradually strengthening. I began to find myself in possession of more than was requisite for our daily wants. I had no debts – I had paid off all the expenses attendant upon my call to the bar and had returned the formidable £100 deposit. My home was a place of undisturbed happiness, for which I was mainly indebted to the admirable management and the sweet companionship of my adorable wife.

The society in which I now lived was altogether different from all I had before been acquainted with; my pursuits, my thoughts, and my exertions were of more elevated tone, and my whole soul was filled with thankfulness and hope. I must say something of the personages among whom I lived. Lord Lyndhurst was the first of the many Chancellors I have seen. His public life is so well and universally known that I need say nothing here about it – but what most commanded my admiration was the clear-sighted judgment which he always displayed – the strong good sense

– and a masculine energy which seemed a part of his nature accompanied by an evenness of temper which commanded universal regard.

The Master of the Rolls, Sir William Grant had retired from his office for several years before I was called to the bar but in the years of my clerkship I had frequently been in the Rolls Court while he was sitting there. My attendance at the Judge's Chambers on occasion often took me to Chancery Lane in the evening – and it was a great pleasure to me to look in at the Rolls where the gravity and decorum which characterized the place were very striking. Three or four of the best leaders – a few only of the outer bar – a sprinkling of attorneys – and no public. He had the well-earned reputation of being an excellent judge, the proofs of which remain in the reports of his judgment. He usually sat at the Rolls Court in the evenings. It was said he had borne arms in his earliest years. He had practiced as a lawyer in Canada and for aught I ever heard had but little practice in England and that chiefly at the cock pit (Privy Council) before his elevation to the Bench, but he was unquestionably of first-rate ability. His appearance was striking – a large figure – remarkably handsome face as Sir Thomas Lawrence's portrait shows most vividly. His taciturnity during the argument might well be imitated by some of the judges I have seen, but the clear forcible style of his decision could not be surpassed. It was said that (not withstanding the freshness of his complexion at a very advanced age) he was a powerful drinker. There may be some truth in the saying for he was one of the giants of those days in which drinking seems to have been a prevalent habit – but it cannot be truly said that he exhibited any external indication of such a propensity. He sat at six in the evening and remained until the case before him was concluded, often as late as nine o'clock and sometimes later – and did not dine until after he rose. It was whispered (but upon no better authority than Dan Wakefield's) that after the cloth was removed his butler placed a bottle of Madeira and a bottle of port upon the table. The servants then went to bed. At what hour the Master of the Rolls retired no one knew – but in the morning each of the bottles was found to be empty.

Sir William Grant was succeeded at the Rolls by Sir Thomas Plumer. On his death in 1824, Lord Gifford was appointed – and Sir John Leach (who was Vice Chancellor at the time of my call) became Master of the Rolls in May 1827. I do not recollect that I had much if any experience of any of these judges except the last who continued in his office till 1834 and who had the reputation of being generally ungracious to the bar and especially to juniors.

At the end of 1827, Sir Lancelot Shadwell became Vice Chancellor of England and continued to occupy that post until his death in 1850, and it was principally in his court that my practice lay and in which I may say that all my experience at the bar was gained.

Vice Chancellor Shadwell was upon the whole a satisfactory judge. He had done reasonably well at Eton and at the University. He was a good scholar as far as being acquainted with the books in which he had been taught went – and he was generally acquainted with the law as it had been administered in the Court of Chancery since the days of Lord Hardwicke – but beyond that circle "he never leant to stray." With literature in its larger and proper sense he had no acquaintance, and although I don't doubt that he could scan and construe Greek and Latin as well as – perhaps better than – any man in his court, he knew nothing and cared no more for the light and instruction which he might have derived from the stores of European learning which were within the reach of a man of ordinary intelligence. He was remarkably good tempered and not impatient. His principal fault was that of being a head-boy – at school and in the world he sustained that character and all the days of his life maintained the character of a school-boy, a lover of fair play in general – but with a slight propensity to a love of mischief, and an unreasonable respect for the bigger boys. A judge who is in any degree in awe of any part of his bar is grievously handicapped. Shadwell had a very able body of seniors before him – and with no desire to disparage his unquestionable merits I cannot help thinking that he did – not unfrequently – pay greater deference to some of them than was always merciful, some of them than was just to them or to himself. He was not unjust to juniors – on the contrary he was always merciful, sometimes indulgent to them – but he could not endure their daring to dispute the authority of opposing leaders – and was inclined to treat their want of deference as a kind of rebellion – if not of high treason. Upon the whole, I believe that there never has been a judge who more diligently and faithfully discharged his duties – and for myself I am bound to say that at all times I received kind and encouraging treatment from him.

His bar was for all public purposes and for the dispatch of business admirably supplied. The most eminent of the practitioners was Sir Edward Sugden. With very slender advantages of education, he had raised himself from a very low social condition. He was thoroughly master of all the law which it was his lot to deal with practically, and possessed besides good sense, and a high spirit nourished by no inconsiderable vanity and self-reliance – and had attained with remarkable rapidity a very high position. He was, by accident, low-bred, by nature imperious and hard hearted, and I don't think he ever had a friend except on Norton who was his devoted toady.

Mr. Bell (Jockey Bell as he was familiarly called), of older and longer standing, had been outstripped by him in the estimation of the attorneys. He was a great favourite with Lord Eldon, who estimated highly his profound knowledge of law – and honoured his upright character and amiable qualities. Without a particle of gracefulness in manners of diction – talking in coarse Northumbrian dialect, his argumentative powers were admirable. Good-natured, accessible, friendly, he was held in high esteem by the attorneys – respected by his fellows – and adored by the juniors. I believe he had made a large fortune at the bar, mostly I think by accumulation, for his habits were very simple. He had grown old, and as I have said, was not in a large practice as he had been for a series of years, and died shortly after I became acquainted with him.

A very lumbering large old man named Agar appeared but seldom. As I heard he had once been famous – a gentleman by birth – the owner of a large tract of land in the fields between Somers Town and Kentish Town. Dan Wakefield declared that he had seen him at a State Ball at the Court of Tuscany dressed in a suit of peach colored satin – a spectacle which we found difficult to reconcile with the appearance which the old gentleman exhibited in our time in the dingy Court at Lincoln's Inn.

Sir Charles Wetherell appeared occasionally but at uncertain intervals – and never but on occasions of a somewhat political kind. I was his junior in a case relating to some Ludlow Charities – in which some members of the corporation took a somewhat radical view of the subject

Lord Lyndhurst as Chancellor was dead against us – I then thought most unrighteously – but he was at least as likely to be right in law as we argued on the contrary. Wetherell was a remarkable man – slovenly in appearance – indolent – absent of mind very commonly – but when roused, of most extraordinary power – full of learning of all kinds – and master of the abundant burning rhetoric which though it often failed to convince his hearers never failed to command their admiration. Perhaps he was a little mad (I have seldom known any man of exalted intellect who was not a little mad). But that he possessed extraordinary gifts his speeches in the House of Commons – and his conduct of the trial of the prisoners for high treason – furnish irrefragable proofs. He was held in high esteem by the fanatics of the Tory Party – and among others was the cherished friend of the much abused Duke of Cumberland and King of Hanover, who sued to pay him frequent visits in his chambers in Stone Buildings. I was sitting late one evening with Billy Wright in his chambers in Stone Buildings when there came a knock at the outer door. It was Wetherell, who, knowing that Wright had some famous Staffordshire Ale (rare stuff it was), came to beg for a bottle with which he wished to regale his visitor – the Duke of Cumberland. Wright gave him two bottles, which he carried off for the Duke – and I have no reason to doubt that they were duly dispatched.

Wetherell's Chambers were a sight not to be forgotten. One of the largest rooms on the ground floor – they had once been handsomely furnished – with large mirrors, gilded armchairs, console table, etc. But the Chambers had not been painted, nor even whitewashed for many years – all was dirty and in decay. Upon the marble top of the gilded table lay Wetherell's Court suit – velvet coat and breeches – shoes and buckles an inch thick in dust – papers, letters, books, scattered in heedless profusion. At the end of the room a partition formed by folding doors within which lay his bed – a deplorable little four-poster with hangings which once had been white. I was once summoned to a consultation with him. It was during the debate on the Reform Bill in 1832. His faithful clerk showed us into the large room – and told us (in confidence) that his master had come very late – or early – and was in bed but would soon be with us. We waited (that is I and the client, who was the little radical Lord Mayor, Wire) for at least a quarter of an hour when, after we had proposed to the clerk that we should come at some more convenient opportunity, the doors were suddenly thrown open and Wetherell came out in his nightshirt. He – nothing abashed – said "Oh! It is you – come in," and threw himself back on his bed – decently drawing the sheet over him. We approached – not without some awe – and then and there we had our consultation. That he had read his brief there could be no doubt – for he knew the case perfectly – told us we were sure to win – as within about an hour, with his help – we did. I forget the particulars – but it was thought to be somewhat difficult and involved the right of one of the city companies to an estate which had become valuable subject to some eleemosynary trust. He dismissed the attorney but asked me to wait a few minutes while he dressed. He immediately put on a dressing gown and proceeded to shave. His toilet apparatus was of the simplest kind – upon the shelf of a very handsome mantel piece of carved Carrara marble stood a small pot with soap in it – and a well-worn brush. Against the wall was a piece of broken looking glass and a dilapidated razor lay behind it. With this, he shaved himself rapidly, certainly and steadily – not at all like a man who had been up the greater part of the night – and without any other preparation (washing was out of the question) he huddled on his clothes and we went together to the Vice Chancellor's Court, where in a very short time we utterly demolished one of Joe Parkes's famous charitable establishments. Poor Joe, by the help of his radical friends in Parliament, had worked himself into a very lucrative practice in these matters. Like the judge in Rabelais (Bridoye the Elder), he never compromised a case until the costs had reached a respectable amount – then he was open to an offer. The City attorneys were not unwilling to stay a frivolous litigation – as most of them were the corpus – means were found for coming to an arrangement which put an end to the dispute upon some pretext which did not seem wholly unreasonable. The founders of the Charity had been in their graves for centuries – direct objects of their bounty had ceased to exist for many generations: "*Il y a des accommodements avec le ciel.*" And peace was happily restored at the expense of the Charity – and to the satisfaction of the belligerent parties. Joe's pocket was often the fuller for the transaction

– but there was an unlucky hole in Joe's pocket which let slip a large proportion of his gains.

I find it difficult to recollect the names of the leaders in Shadwell's Court when I first knew it. There were several men of note in their day. Heald – a stubborn, coarse Lincolnshire man in very full business of the more ordinary kind, much patronized by the attorneys whose faithful energetic servant he always was. Bold, noisy, and clever. An old gentleman named Benyon held his own gentle sway by tradition than by any present power.

Sir Anthony Hart, a most formidable, austere looking old gentleman with very black eyebrows and spectacles with blacker horn rims, filled my soul with awe but I know nothing of him save that he was the leader of the Chancery Bar, was universally esteemed and was afterwards Lord Chancellor of Ireland. Jockey Bell had ceased to practice but was an occasional visitor to the Courts as amicus and always welcomed.

Sir Arthur Pigott appeared very rarely – and never, as I believe, but upon some merely formal business. He was quite an old man but of great reputation. He was treated always with marked respect by the judge and the bar – and by the younger members with a sort of veneration. His figure and appearance were too striking to be forgotten – very tall – and quite upright though nearly seventy years old. He lived in his chambers in the Temple, and used to walk up, through Bell Alley, in his silk gown and full-length wig – with his three-cornered hat in his hand, bowing and bowed to throughout his profess, and took his seat in court like an Emperor. He was certainly a grand old man to look upon. His fame had been established in Parliament, and in the higher tribunals. He was a most earnest and powerful Whig of the old school – and he was looked upon by his party as the safest adviser and a profound statesman. He drew up at the request of his political friends a very remarkable document in the shape of a petition by the widow and children of Lord Edward Fitzgerald to King George III against the Bill of Attainder which had been passed in 1799 – and it was not until 1819 that the attainder was repealed. The petition is an admirable production and justifies all that Moore says of it in his life of Lord Edward Fitzgerald, where he describes it "as a composition more admirable for its purpose – more precious as an example of the adroitness and power with which rhetoric and logic may be made sub-servient to each other – has rarely perhaps been written." (Vol. 2, p. 245.)

The mention of this remarkable paper leads me to say something about equity drawing, which was for several years my principal occupation. The ordinary forms were usually plain enough – bills for the administration of estates – for the enforcement of contracts – ordinary trusts – or partnerships or the great variety of transactions which found their way into the Court of Chancery might be easily dealt with – precedents were very numerous – and a thick volume in print entitled "The Equity Draftsman" furnished a store of forms and phrases readily accessible – but in cases of difficulty or complexity the framing of the pleadings was often of vital importance. To state facts clearly – and in such order and sequence as made the prayer of a bill the logical, irresistible conclusion from the facts, often required a care and foresight which the forms of the precedents did not greatly assist. In answers the opportunity which was furnished to the deft of explaining or qualifying the allegations against him – and of stating the denials and more especially the grounds upon which he relied for defence, was of the utmost value. In such cases, and they were not infrequent, precedents were almost worthless but the study and contemplation of such a petition as Sir Arthur Pigott's sere of inestimable value.

The recent alterations of the practice in Chancery have wholly abolished the art of drawing. Any intelligent attorney's clerk can draw a claim and as matters now stand under the improved (?) rules, a summons. No defendant need commit himself by answering – he may of course allege and prove by evidence whatever his grounds of defence may be – but always without the simplicity and certainty of the former system. No doubt much greater dispatch has been attained, perhaps in many cases the expense has been diminished although that seems questionable – but that litigation has been greatly encouraged and increased appears to me to be unquestionable. Cases of the most trumpery kind now occupy the Court of Chancery, though they might be better disposed of at the court of piepowders.

I have known many cases that have been won or lost mainly upon the pleading. For although the judges cannot be justly accused of having given any very careful or critical attention upon the mere pleadings, they could not fail, in cases which brought out the very points in issue in plain and convincing force, to bestow due consideration upon the subject. In drawing cases of appeal to the House of Lords the skill of the draughtsman had full scope – for although of course it was not permitted to add to, or alter, or in any manner to colour the facts as they had been argued and decided upon in the Courts below, there was no rule preventing the statements of the points which had been the subject of decision, and I have known instances in which the use of italics, in the printed cases, has at least had the effect of preventing the possibility of such points being disregarded on appeal. Another valuable result of discreet pleading was that it not infrequently led to compromises in cases (by no means infrequent) in which, as Sir Roger de Coverley was wont to say, there was "much to be said on both sides" because in such cases the scientific construction of the mere pleading has enabled the parties interested to understand and reflect upon the true force and weight of the subject of the dispute and the limits of their respective interests.

Although in the particular cases I have alluded to I cannot but regret that the very great value of pleading has been lost sight of, I am not forgetful that very great improvements have been introduced. The six clerks, the sixty Clerks in the Court – Masters in Chancery – and a crowd of useless officers – and unmeaning and costly forms have been utterly abolished to the substantial relief of the suitors – and to the triumph of common sense. I cannot, however, but regret the destruction of the essential *narratio* – nor approve of the miserable claim which was substituted for it – and the writ or summons which has taken its place.

In this desultory story which I have been telling I have been led away from the account which I had intended to give of the Court of Chancery when I first knew it. Besides the leaders I have named, there were many men behind the bar who had given promise of great ability and who upon the accession of the new Lord Chancellor were eager aspirants of the much desired silk gowns which Lord Eldon so sparingly distributed. Among them were Mr. Pepys (afterwards Lord Cottenham), Pemberton

(Lord Kingsdown), Knight Bruce – a coarse, rough Lincolnshire man, Heald – of ability and great practice – George Turner – James Wigram – Kindersley – Jacob, one of the ablest and best tempered of men – whose early death alone prevented his attaining the highest honours. (I am afraid I have mentioned some of these before). All these men (but not all together) came to the front – Sugden remained, tyrant and master of all, until he became Chancellor of Ireland on the death of Sir Anthony Hart.

It is among the most agreeable of my recollections that by all these men I was treated with kindness and regard for which I cannot be sufficiently thankful, while the pleasure of their conversation and society was the delight of my life. From each of them I experienced encouragement, and from their example instruction, to which I owe all the success I have enjoyed.

Among them one whom I esteemed most highly was James Parker – who was afterwards Vice Chancellor, and whose premature death deprived the public and the profession of a most able and efficient judge – and his family and friends of one and the most dear and valued beings that ever existed. At his house in the Regents Park I met several notable persons – among whom that one I recollect best was [Thomas Babington] Macauley – then recently returned from India. All that I distinctly remember of him was that his conversation was the most remarkable event of the evening and that it hardly displayed any of those "streaks of silence" which Sidney Smith said were now sometimes observable in him.

It was the constant practice in those days for all, or almost all, the barristers in Chancery to go to Chambers in the evenings. It was indeed the only time in which men who had drawing to do, or briefs to read could bestow upon their work such uninterrupted labour as their tasks required. Parker's Chambers were not far from mine and it had become a habit with him to knock at my door when he was departing (seldom before midnight) and invite me to walk homeward with him as far as our routes went together. I remember that on one occasion a case of very considerable importance had been partly heard before Shadwell and stood for reply on the following day. Bethell, who was Parker's leader, had, of course, to reply. On coming out of Court, Parker said to me "I don't think Bethell means to reply. I have asked him and he assures me that he will be in his place tomorrow but I suspect he means to play me false." I did not think it possible and did my best to calm his doubts. But it turned out that he knew his man better than I then did. At sometime after twelve at night, Parker came into my Chambers with a note from Bethell which had been dropped a few minutes before into his letter box (the outer door was always closed when the clerk went away). It was dated at eight o'clock tomorrow morning – and gave a pitiable account of the illness of Lady Bethell, with whom the writer had been sitting up all night, and who was still in such a dangerous condition that he could not leave her – and he was to his great regret obliged to ask Parker to reply for him. Bethell's clerk had no doubt been ordered to leave the letter early in the morning, and to save himself the trouble of early rising, and to make sure that the note would reach Parker in good time, had dropped it into the box before it purported to have been written.

I afterwards learnt that Bethell had played a similar trick with De Boots. I don't think it is much worthwhile telling because Bethell's aptitude at lying became so notorious that none but idiots ever believed a word he said.

A life of Lord Westbury has lately (Nov. 1888) been published by a Mr. Nash. I have not seen it – but from such notices of it as I have seen in the reviews it would seem not to be highly interesting. I don't see how it could be. Perhaps at some other time I may add to this note. His talents, though of a very limited kind, were undoubtedly considerable, so far as they went, and his audacity almost heroic. I don't think that he had many friends – or that he tried to make or keep any. Of his personal character, as I have little to say in his praise, I may as well remain silent.

Scotland

But what is worth telling if I could recollect it all is a voyage I made with Parker to the Hebrides. (Note of October 27, 1888: I had written so far in the early part of the summer when I became very unwell. Sis took me in at Sudbury, where I remained until the following August. Then Frank took me to Compton where the Shees were visiting us. They left us at the end of their fortnight's visit. Lydia and Nelly and Susan and Jem then joined us and they stayed till the middle of September – Sis came for a few days

– and then they all departed – the younger ones to their respective schools – Tertius and Sis and the two elder girls to proceed upon their holiday travels. Their first destination was towards the South of France – bur an unlucky fit of gout attacked Tertius at Pau and detained them there for several days. They afterwards got to Biarritz – and have since been making excursion in that neighbourhood but the notion which Sis had been entertaining of reaching Madrid has been sadly disappointed. They have, however, seen Fontarabia and San Sebastian, which Sis says she finds wonderfully different from what she recollects of them in a former excursion which she made with me (in happier days!) now four and thirty years ago. They may yet perhaps get a glimpse of some of the places in the Pyrenees – the mountains and the foliage must needs be worth seeing in this autumnal sunshine. We (Frank, Aunt Fanny and I) stayed at Compton till the end of September, when his duties called him to London, and here we have since remained. Compton was pleasant enough, the weather good, but very cold winds – they did not, however, interfere much with the lawn tennis parties by which Frank enlivened our solitude. The weather during the so-called summer has not been favourable to the rheumatism with which I have been and am grievously tormented. Walking is out of the question – the Doctors (Swinhoe and Aikin) both confess they can do nothing for me – and decline to give me any medicine – or prescribe any other remedies than rubbing and warmth and quiet. So I must "grin and bear it" as well as I may and thank God that it is no worse. The winter has set in – the fogs have begun their diversions – the sunshine, when it appears, is a bright mockery and the days are very short. Here ends this digression and I resume my original story.)

My trip to the Hebrides has left very agreeable recollections – I joined the party at Gourock on the Clyde, a country house of Major Darrock, who was married to a sister of Parker. I suppose the estate was a considerable one – the house large and commodious, the grounds extensive – the river views agreeable. In a corner of the policy (as it called in Scotland) was the family burial place – so retired and so thickly planted about as to be almost concealed – but strewed with tombs – and strikingly solemn and affecting when its recesses were penetrated. Much more impressive than our more usual Southern Church Yards – but a little startling to our superstitions.

Parker had hired from the Clyde Yacht Club the Commodore's boat, a vessel of 80 tons burden. An experienced old captain, with half a dozen able seamen. The ship was admirably found in all respects, and with sufficient accommodation for Parker, his wife, two daughter and two sons, all pleasant and cheerful. I don't recollect our exact course – our first trip was to Campbell Town and thence passing in fair weather the formidable whirlpool of Corrie Verchen, threaded the series of islands – the sound of Mull – the point of Ardnamurchan – Rum and Egg – and all the places mentioned in Dr. Johnson's Tour, and some of the most striking of the scenes described in Scott's Lord of the Isles. All these have been so often told that it would not be worthwhile to dwell upon them here, even if my remembrance of their details were more vivid than, I am sorry to confess, it is. It is impossible however to forget the wild beauty of Loch Seawig, where our boat was joined by a smaller boat containing a brother of Parker's – with his wife and two charming little girls – and another Archie Smith (who was some years afterwards married Parker's youngest daughter). To these was added another yacht belonging to a Captain _____, a friend of Parker. In this wild land-locked little bay we stayed a couple of days, catching large trawls of seatrout and other fish, and greatly disturbing a number of solemn lazy black-eyed seals who disported themselves on the rocks and in the waters and which baffled or defied Captain _____'s gun.

Here we landed and explored the wild rocky pass of Coruisk; a most Dantesque spectacle. Vincent's unfinished sketch of Coruisk, recalls the savagery of the scene. Archie Smith had provided himself – with a portable India-rubber boat which, inflated by a pair of bellows, was capable of carrying safely two persons – and in which he had the skill to navigate the dismal waters of this most doleful lake and, more remarkable, Mrs. Parker had the courage to accompany him in his voyage. We visited Staffa in very favorable weather and were able by means of the dingey to land at the entrance to the cavern [i.e. Fingal's Cave] and to clamber along the somewhat rugged paths (if the broken masses of stone can be called a path) to the very end. The bright sunshine displayed the tall, basaltic columns and their varying colours, with admirable effects of light and shade – the lofty arch with its pendant stalactites resounded with the voices of the wild waves tossed in by the tide – and, when the surface of the watery floor was in patches undisturbed, the abundant vegetation, the seaweed added a charm to the scene. It would be difficult to imagine a more striking object than this wild dismantled ruined cathedral, formed by nature, and apparently destined to last in its present condition as long as the world shall subsist.

After a lengthened visit to this stupendous scene, we visited Iona – landed – explored the ruins of that most ancient shrine of learning and piety – and then returned to our hospitable ship.

We made many other trips and were delighted with all we saw. One of our visits was to the island of Raisey – the property of a kinsman of Parker – Mr. Rainery, who, having made a considerable fortune in China, laid out a large sum in the purchase of this island, which as I afterwards learned, did not turn out wholly advantageous – for on the failure of a harvest the laird found himself burdened with the duty of maintaining the whole population who must otherwise have starved. When I saw the island, all was fairly prosperous – and our visit was especially to celebrate the christening of a newly born son of the laird. A large company was assembled on the occasion and the ceremony was rendered the more solemn inasmuch as the sacred rite was performed by a minister who had been a traveler and a missionary and who brought with him a bottle of water of the river Jordan.

After three weeks of most agreeable journeying, we returned to the Clyde, where our party broke up and I, after a visit to Edinburgh, went home and I thought – and I think still – that Edinburgh as well from its natural features as from its varied associations, is one of the most interesting places I have ever beheld.

Home and Leading Legal Personalities

It is by no means my intention to chronicle my progress at the bar of the Court of Chancery. I had the good fortune to get into a good practice not, of course without occasional disappointment – but at all times most happy in a home which was the seat of the purest delight and which prevented me from repining at the unavoidable sorrows and checks which are common to the lot of humanity but which it would be most unprofitable and ungrateful to recall. Still less ought I here to indulge in lamentations over what can never be forgotten. I may however mention that my course was not without temptations. After the passing of the Reform Bill, the road to Parliament being widely opened, many persons at the bar had strong inclinations and inducements to enter upon that hazardous and slippery career. Mr. Walter (the old man), who had a too favorable opinion of my ability, came to me in Lincoln's Inn and urged me strongly to offer myself as a candidate for a borough in the Isle of Wight where, as we believed, the chance of my being returned was most favorable. I had begun as I thought to "take hold of the ground" in the Court of Chancery – I was strongly tempted – but I had given pledges to Fortune – I was in all senses fortunate and supremely happy. I discussed it with the dear partner of my joys – who was at first inclined that I should run the risk – but whom I at length succeeded in persuading that we ought not to imperil what we had gained by striving after what might be a failure. I was afraid – so, which many hearty thanks to Mr. Walter I declined his generous offer, and his most friendly advice. I cannot hope that I convinced him of the propriety of my determination – for upon my suggesting to him that the qualification for a member (it was then an actual income of £300 a year) was far beyond my means, he said that should be no difficulty for that he would readily furnish it. So I continued to plod – and I am bound to say that I have had no reason to regret my determination.

Another great temptation beset me in the early part of my upward career. An unusual number of railway undertakings were brought forward and the practice before parliamentary committees presented great inducements to all practitioners. The fees were of enormous amount compared with the remuneration afforded by the Courts in the ordinary course of business. I had the good fortune to be retained by the Ayr and Calder Navigation Company, whose vital interests were assailed and endangered by the North Country Railroad Companies. Many were the fights – and long – and sometimes hot and angry, in which I was engaged, single-handed, against the favoured few who, having relinquished general business, had devoted themselves to this most lucrative and by no means difficult branch of practice. They had besides the advantage of having gained what is called the *ear* of the committees – and as the promoters were discreet enough to hold out the prospect of future gain (if not of present substantial advantage) to land owners whose influence with the committees was hardly concealed, all that the opponents, my clients, could hope for was to insist upon such qualification and conditions as would save them from absolute spoliation. To some extent – if not wholly satisfactorily – my clients succeeded in averting the ruin with which they were threatened. I believe they were thankful to have made the best of a bad bargain. I made five or six hundred pounds in a few weeks, more than treble what I could have earned in the Court of Chancery, – my business in which did not suffer from such temporary absence as was occasioned by my parliamentary exertions. Charles Austen and Wrangham made large fortunes before committees – both men of unquestionable ability – and they were succeeded with nearly equal good fortune by Mr. Burke an attorney's clerk – and Mr. Denison, now Lord Grimthorpe, who had tried the Court of Chancery with indifferent success. So that although I never hesitated to admit that Austen and Wrangham were men of great ability, I was more inclined to ascribe their eminent success to chance and good fortune than to their personal qualifications. Right or wrong, I determined to have nothing to do with committees and although I had very tempting offers from Mr. Leach managing the Railway Bill for Swain and Stevens (one of the partners, the energetic Mr. Hunt was particularly civil to me), I refused to accept any briefs in Parliament and determined to abide by "my hollow tree – my crust of bread and liberty" in the Court of Chancery.

I must try to recollect some of the remarkable personages with whom I became more or less acquainted in my career. When I was called to the bar, Lord Lyndhurst had succeeded Lord Eldon as Chancellor – and his practice having been chiefly – if not wholly – confined to the Courts of Common Law it was suggested – perhaps not unnaturally – that it was not likely that he would adequately supply the place of his great predecessor. The result proved that the intellectual power that Lord Lyndhurst unquestionably possessed was more than sufficient for the discharge of his new duties and I do not think that in the long roll of Chancellors any more able judge is to be found. (I am afraid there is some repetition here of what I have written in earlier pages – but it must be excused). Considering the unimportant and uninteresting nature of much of what he had to do, it may be doubted whether such talents as he possessed were not infrequently more than the occasion required. No judge could be more attentive to the subject before him – none more quick in collecting the really important points, and in discriminating and dismissing the chaff from the grain, while the accuracy with which he retained and recapitulated (when the occasion required it) the most complicated statements of dates, amounts, and facts was most remarkable – and all this without taking notes, and without the slightest tincture of affectation or show. He was sometimes accused of being indifferent and callous – but I think most unjustly so accused and I well remember a case in which this stern and iron-looking man was so moved by the case before him that he fairly broke down in sobs while delivering his judgment. I forget the names – but the question was as to the validity of something which had been attempted by a father against the rights of an only child, a daughter, for whom he had previously entertained the fondest affection – but who had so displeased him by marrying against his wishes, that he had conceived an aversion amounting to hatred against her. The decision was against the validity of the transaction and that upon the ground that the father had evinced a hatred of his daughter (against whom no other misconduct was alleged than her marriage without the parent's consent) as amounted to insanity.

     The case made a sensation – and much discussion arose upon the most difficult question of "partial insanity" – but the decision remained and was generally approved of. I wish I had the means (which I have not at present) of stating the matter more particularly – but I well recollect the substance and the most impressive judgment – and the emotion which the judge displayed. After little less than four years, the political change which ensued compelled him to relinquish in 1830 the seat which however twice (in 1835 and 1841) he afterwards regained, having in the meantime been appointed Chief Baron of the Exchequer.[2] His history has been written and I am not called upon here to repeat any part of it – but I do not hesitate to

---

[2] A medieval office, abolished in 1875 and replaced by the Exchequer Division and, from 1880, the King's Bench Division of the High Court

place him in the first rank of all the great men I have seen and besides all this he gave me my silk gown [i.e. promoted me to King's Counsel] in June 1846.

Lyndhurst was succeeded in 1830 by the turbulent Lord Brougham, who came into his office breathing threats and promises about the extirpation of existing abuses in the Court of Chancery and the introduction of useful reforms. Many abuses he did no doubt extinguish – the reforms he contemplated – and many others were left to wiser heads and more accomplished hands. It cannot be denied that he was very clever man – knowing much – daring, strong, impudent and without any steadfast principle – his best qualities were shorn of their true value by his egregious vanity. His popularity once fairly earned, was marred by his own willfulness – and he had become so intolerable to his friends and adherents that when he went out of office in November 1834, his fall was not regretted by anyone but himself and his immediate adherents.

It must be confessed that Brougham's advent to the Court of Chancery was not regarded with much cordiality by the practitioners there. Sugden, then *facile princeps* of the leaders, did not attempt to conceal his contempt for Brougham's pretentions to know anything of the duties of the office into which he had intruded – or even his title to that little degree of knowledge of law of which, it was said, if he could have added that little to his other stores would have made him an Admirable Crichton, or a Pico della Mirandola. Consequently, they were not upon agreeable terms. The like feeling of distrust pervaded the whole of the practicing bar, and with the exception of a few expectants I doubt whether any Chancellor had fewer friends among the practitioners of Lincoln's Inn.

It must be admitted that he did not make any effort to commend himself to his new acquaintances. He was not angry or tyrannous – but he was insolent and ill-bred. They had been used to treat the Lord Chancellor with a sort of respect, if not of reverence. He broke through all forms – disregarded rules which they felt bound to observe. The last thing he permitted himself to consider were the customs and habits which they considered essential parts of the system. In his eagerness to dispatch business (some of which was greatly in arrear) he prolonged sitting to unreasonable hours – inconvenient to all persons concerned: not only to the officers and attendants on the Court, who having discharged their daily duties had earned their night's rest – but to counsel, some of whom were in the habit of working for long hours after the public business of the day had been concluded. Among his eccentricities, he appointed evening sittings of hearing appeals from the Vice Chancellors and the Rolls Courts. This was before the establishment of the Court of Appeal. I remember looking into the Old Lincolns Inn Hall one night at about eleven o'clock when I found Bethell addressing the slumbering Chancellor, with two or three other Counsel, half asleep, and with no other audience than some of the vagrants from Chancery Lane who had doubtless been attracted by the light and warmth of the hall.

Upon another occasion a scene occurred which created some sensation, though it did not attract public attention beyond the precincts of Lincoln's Inn, probably because none of the press reporters were present. The Court, which on this occasion sat at 8 o'clock, was attended by a good many counsel. The appeal was in a commercial case of importance and was of some length; parties as well as counsel were present, among them a French advocate who seemed to take great interest in the proceedings.

Lord Brougham, (who had dined) addressed himself to the hearing with all becoming gravity – but was evidently somewhat oppressed. He sent for snuff and had handed to him a brilliant tin box filled with Lundy Foot's famous snuff, with which he plentifully regaled his very remarkable nose. After a time, he gave himself up to a slumber which Lundy Foot could not dispel ... Sir William Horne was arguing. Whether he exercised a narcotic influence on the judge or his previous exertions overpowered him who can say? The French gentleman was almost frantic at hearing the audible snore uttered by the Chancellor. He rose up and exclaimed, "*Ne peut-on pas éveiller le Juge?*" Le Marchant, the Secretary, who was sitting at the table, clutched Brougham's gown and succeeded, not without difficulty, in awaking him. Lord Brougham, with that ready and cool impudence that never deserted him, merely shook himself, took another pinch of snuff, and said to Horne, "Go on Sir William." Immediately after this, some counsel suggested that it might be expedient to adjourn the further hearing, and this being joined in by most of the Bar – and perhaps assisted by some whisper from Le Marchant, the Chancellor with apparent reluctance assented. The case was afterwards peacefully heard – and I have no reason to doubt that it was properly decided – but to the best of my recollection this was the last of the night sittings.

Sir John Leach was Master of the Rolls from 1827 to his death in 1834, when he was succeeded by Sir Christopher Pepys. I suppose no judge was ever more generally or more deservedly disliked than Leach. Clever and quick, but with slender knowledge of the law he was entrusted to administer, he was believed to owe his preferment to his subserviency to Court influence – and especially to the Prince Regent,[3] with whom he was a great favorite. In the House of Commons (he sat for the rotten borough of Seaford), he defended the Duke of York,[4] and was afterwards, as it was said, actively engaged in getting up the infamous evidence adduced in the House of Lords against Queen Caroline. That he was of humble extraction is no doubt true. He had been in the employment of Taylor the eminent Architect. Dan Wakefield (whom it would not be safe to swear after) declared that he knew him, when he was acting as "Clerk of the Works" at the building of stone buildings erected by Taylor. He afterwards turned to the Law, practiced at Common Law and Session; got into business in Equity; was made Chancellor of the Duchy of Cornwall; and soon afterwards Chief Justice of Chester. From 1818 to 1827, he was Vice Chancellor, and thenceforward to his death he held the office of Master of the Rolls. His decisions, prompt and confident as they always were, were not respected, and are now seldom referred to as authorities. His demeanour towards the Bar was always insolent and arbitrary. He had no friends and no favorites but Pemberton, who, being the nephew of Mr. Cooks (the colleague of Leach in getting up the case against the poor Queen), was always treated by him graciously, but whose ability and merit very soon showed that he could soar upon his own wings and who became the absolute Monarch at the Rolls. George Turner and [Sir Richard Torin] Kindersley were his only competitors, and such was his unquestionable superiority that they (although they were both men of great ability) could

---

[3] The future King George IV (r. 1820-1830) reigned as Prince Regent for a decade before his accession.
[4] The future King William IV (r. 1830-1837)

hardly be called his rivals, while Leach's ferocity to others was mollified towards him by whom his spirit was evidently rebuked.

On Brougham's departure at the end of 1834, the Great Seal was put into commission. Pepys, Master of Rolls at the head; Shadwell, Vice Chancellor; and Rolfe (Lord Cranworth) being the other Commissioners. In January 1836, Pepys received the Great Seal and, being Chancellor, was created Baron Cottenham. He retained that office and continued to hold it until September 1841, when, his party being turned out, he resigned. He continued, however, to assist in the hearing of appeals in the House of Lords and in the Privy Council until July 1846 when, his party being restored to power, he again became Lord Chancellor and so continued until the end of June 1850 – when under the pressure of severe illness he resigned the office he had held for nearly ten years. He was then created Earl of Cottenham. He travelled on the Continent in the hope of regaining his strength but died at Pietra Santa, in the Duchy of Lucca, on 19 April 1851. I believe he was the only Whig Lord Chancellor, except Lord Cranworth, who of late years has been restored to his place.

I have heard many opinions amongst the members of the Bar respecting his merits as a judge, but my own, founded upon a very close observation of many years is that he was, by far, the best Lord Chancellor I have become acquainted with. I had no very particular acquaintance with him – and my estimate of his character is not in any way influenced by my personal predilection for him. I think the first point which attracted me and afterwards secured my admiration, was the great patience he displayed in Shadwell's Court. His chief opponents then and there were Sugden and Knight Bruce. No doubt they were both very clever and able men – but they were provocative – and Shadwell, though he was not always absolutely unfair, was too ready to listen to positive assertions – while they were not slow to take advantage of the judge's evident bias who lent a more favorable ear to their petulant interruptions. He evinced a partiality which they were not slow to take advantage of. Shadwell did not duly appreciate the merits of Pepys – and did not justly check the annoying and sometimes intemperate objections of his opponents. To all this he opposed a grave and resolute resistance, and never evinced the least disturbance of temper. This gave me a lofty notion of the strength of his mind – for I should say that he was by nature one of the proudest of men. Shadwell was a schoolboy all the days of his life and always on that side which appeared to be the strongest. However, the time was to come when Cottenham the Judge of Appeal was called upon to redress the wrongs which Mr. Pepys had suffered – and I do not think he was forgetful or unwilling to pay off the score.

I have heard it alleged against him that having conceived a strong opinion in favor of one side of the question before him, he gave undue weight to the facts of the case. In my opinion this charge was groundless. The truth is that he discovered not unfrequently that facts which had been neglected or not duly enforced in the course of the discussion furnished satisfactory grounds on which the rightful decision ought to be based. He was a perfect master of his craft. With no rhetorical skill, he talked with remarkable accuracy of expression – reasoned loudly – and drew irresistibly accurate conclusions – and maintained the authority of the law and the dignity of the tribunal over which he presided in a greater degree than any of the great judges of his time – and in his time there were great judges.

In saying that he was a proud man, I do not mean that there was anything austere or forbidding in his manner or his conversation. On the contrary, he was perfectly cheerful and good tempered. He was not unwilling to listen to or take share in a joke – at least while he was in Shadwell's Court – for after that he was too far removed for any familiar conversation. He was my client on one occasion in the course of my Surrey Sessions practice, although he was quite unconscious of it. He occupied a charming villa at Combe Wood – where I more than once had occasion to wait upon him for, or against, injunctions in the Vacations. The views towards Epsom commanding the Downs were charming. One of his stable boys had stolen a headstall or some other article of harness, and the coachman had hauled him up before the magistrate by whom he was committed for trial at the Sessions. The case was a clear one and notwithstanding Montagu Chambers's eloquent defense, I persuaded the jury to find him guilty, and he was sent to gaol for two months. The matter was altogether new to Mr. Pepys, and I had the pleasure of making him acquainted for the first time with some of the economic arrangements of his stable and making him laugh at some of the incidents of the trial.

He was supposed by some people – who of course did not know much of his habits – to know or care for nothing beyond the law. This was a great mistake – he was a good scholar – and in all respects a man of cultivated mind. His advocacy was without an attempt at ornament, but with his pen he was a master of pure English style as evinced by many of his judgments. I was his junior in a copyright case. A naturalist had produced an elaborate treatise on butterflies – published by subscription – with colored plates and much prized by dilettanti and sold at half-guinea prices. A poor paste and scissors bookmaker named Mudie had had the audacity to produce a half-crown book on the same mysterious subject, and, as it seemed many persons were interested in the pursuit, Mudie's book was so far successful that it alarmed Mr. Stephens, who invoked the Court of Chancery to restrain by injunction this which he called an invasion of his rights. The case could only be properly investigated by a comparison of the two publications. We battled it for some time before Vice Chancellor Shadwell. Everybody found it tedious – and at length the leaders agreed that it would be right to refer it to the arbitration or reference of a learned Seni or Wrangler named Brandreth in the Temple and so it was disposed of for the time. Our case was that it was no piracy although we admitted that we had consulted Mr. Stephens and other works – but we had not copied. As we were typing up our papers Mr. Pepys said to me "You will have to go to Brandreth. Don't forget to quote Swift to him. If in one couplet he can fix the sense of what I put in six, if with much genius, fate has blest him. Have I not reason to detest him?" After two or three sittings, Brandreth was convinced that there was no plagiarism, but real work by client, and Mr. Stephens had to pay the costs.

Mudie was literally a bookmaker. He had a small house at Camberwell – and had engaged half a dozen or more scribblers, male and female, who came to his workshop daily. They breakfasted together at 8 o'clock, dined at one, had tea at 6, and left off at 8, when they departed to such several homes as they had. The intervals they employed in transcribing and compiling and thus prepared, under Mudie's editorship, a variety of treatises, historical, scientific, and others which were sold at very moderate prices, but became popular and were profitable to the editor and the small publishers whom he was engaged with or employed by.

Lord Cottenham went out in 1850 and was succeeded by [Thomas] Wilde (Lord Truro), who remained with us only about two years – a thoroughly able man of great intellectual power, of indefatigable industry, invincible resolution, but knowing of Equity Law "neither text nor margin." He was courteous and even indulgent to the Bar and was remarkably kind and civil to me. I have reason to believe that if he could have had his own way, he would have made me a Vice Chancellor. But at that time Kindersley, who had been displaced with the other Masters in Chancery on their suppression and was in the enjoyment of a pension, was so strongly pressed upon the Chancellor and the government, by Wigram and others, that Wilde was compelled to forego his good intentions in my favor. Kindersley was in all respects a host suitable choice and after a short time the pain I felt at my disappointment wore off, and I went about my work as usual.

In 1852 Sugden became Lord Chancellor and was created Lord St. Leonards. He remained only about a year when he departed upon a change of ministry without making any particular mark, but was, on the whole less, offensive than might have been expected from so disagreeable a person.

Rolfe, who had been appointed Vice Chancellor from the bench of the Exchequer, and who had been created Lord Cranworth, was appointed in 1851 one of the judges of the newly constituted Court of Appeal – and in December 1852 he became Lord Chancellor, an office which he worthily filled for the following five years.

I think I have said enough, for the present at least, about the Chancellors. I have no intention to chronicle my own exploits. The tale would be a dull one – for nothing of remarkable interest occurred to me. My day and, not infrequently, a good part of my night, were spent in sheer hard work, all the day in or about the courts, after dinner back to Chambers. My clerk went away at nine o'clock, the outer door was shut, and I remained at work as long as the occasion required – or as long as I could keep awake, and thus I got well acquainted with the tune of the Old

Hundredth Psalm as it was played at midnight by the chimes of St. Clement Danes.

I gave up, but not until after several years, on all literary exercises, for I had found full employment for all my time in the business that came to me. I must not, however, forget or be ungrateful for the substantial pecuniary help which I had, up to the time I am now referring to, derived from my scribbling. I had furnished political weekly leaders to a Stockport newspaper – articles to several Magazines – translated some French memoirs and novels – and had written many dramatic criticisms for the *Times* and some other newspapers. The pay for all these exertions was not very large but it was helpful. My professional gains, however, became so much more considerable that I could safely throw away the crutches upon which I had hitherto crawled. I had several pupils, each of whom was so infatuated as to pay me 100 guineas for the valuable privilege of seeing how I drew bills and answers and answered the cases submitted for my opinion.

After I became a judge, some feelings, almost remorseful, assailed me when I reflected upon this part of my career and doubted whether my pupils had their money's worth. I felt somewhat like Gil Blas, who, upon visiting, in his mature age, the city in which he had practiced under Dr. Sangrado acknowledges a slight touch of communication, "*Parce que dans ma jeunesse j'y ai exercé la medicine.*" For my first pupil I was indebted to my friend Christie, whose acquaintance I had made and whose society and friendship were most delightful and advantageous to me all the days of his life. Other pupils followed, for I had got a kind of reputation as a draftsman, and pupils like to follow one another, like Panurge's sheep.

Through Christie I became acquainted with J. G. Lockhart then settled in London as editor of the *Quarterly Review*, and at his house, and elsewhere, became acquainted with Campbell, and Galt, and with a John Wilson, a Scotsman who was supposed to be practising in the Court of Chancery – but who was really actively employed in writing some very good novels published in Edinburgh – and a frequent contributor to the then most popular *Blackwood*. Among many very agreeable recollections was a memorable dinner at the Ship at Greenwich with Christie, Lockhart – that most good natured old thirsty law bookseller, Charles Hunter – who had taken to trade after wasting a competent fortune in riotous living in Scotland and who supplied me with books upon the easy terms that I should pay him when he asked me for the price. He never did ask me, but I paid him sooner I believe either he or I expected. Lord Panmure (famous as Fox Maule, and later the 11th Earl of Dalhousie) was Hunter's great friend and patron and was also present. I believe they helped one another to die of hard drinking. Another memorable man, Sir R[obert] Ferguson (See Lockhart's *Life of Scott*), a soldier who had been through the Peninsular War until he was taken prisoner on the blowing up of a bridge in Spain, and for whom Sir Walter Scott, who loved him much, had obtained the post of Keeper of the Regalia of Scotland, which had been accidentally discovered at Holyrood, to the great pride and delight of all Scotland. His good temper and droll stories of his military experiences – especially his residence upon parole during his captivity with a Rabelaisian Cure – were highly diverting, and his charming songs "We'll gang nae mare to yon Town, see late into the night" enlivened one of the most agreeable meetings I ever had a share in.

I could write volumes about the pleasant and good fellows by whom I was surrounded and whose society and friendliness made my life pass very pleasantly. But my time is getting short, and I have more work before me than I am sure I shall be able to accomplish. I must, however, mention some of their names, at least.

Knight Bruce, the great leader, after Sugden and Cottenham had disappeared from the Bar, on being raised to the Bench, was about as good an advocate as I have known or have heard of or read about. His patient and untiring devotion to the task before him would have ensured him eminent success even if they had not been accompanied (as they were) by most remarkable intelligence and rapidity. Not in any proper sense persuasive or rhetorical, he was always clear and, when need was, irresistibly impressive. If there was any law, he did not know about he always took care to learn it before it was required and always had it ready where the occasion called for it. He was not always quite good tempered but he was never tyrannous or offensive – and if he quarreled, it was always upon provocation – and he only quarreled with men whom he thought worthy of his steel. He had, I doubt not, a high, but not too high, opinion of his own worth, and cannot be blamed for thinking (as he must have done) that several persons less able to serve the public in the highest office which the profession could confer had been preferred to him. Nevertheless, it cannot be justly said of him that he suffered his disappointments to interfere with the duties of the several judicial appointments he held – or gave any external sign that he thought he had been unworthily treated.

Wigram and Kindersley were close friends and admirable specimens of the class of gentlemen which ought to characterize the Bar. They were remarkably good looking and were reckoned (not by merely partial observers) to be among the handsomest men in London. They were both in full practice and both well deserved the eminence they attained. Kindersley tired of the Rolls, and perhaps, tired of waiting became a Master in Chancery (for which he was much too good) and Wigram became one of the Vice Chancellors. Kindersley was very fond of music and upon taking possession of his first and only Chambers in Stone Buildings (which he shared for several years with Wigram) had deposited there a handsome grand piano with which he solaced his idle hours before business flowed in upon him. After no long time, however, there was no more playing upon it – and I knew it for many years to be covered with coats of dust which the laundress did not dare to disturb and heavy piles of papers, briefs past and present. Wigram, who, when I knew him first, was very advantageously and happily married and the father of a large family had, it was obscurely hinted, led somewhat of a *jeunesse orageuse*. Fitzroy Stanhope, who had been at Cambridge, with him used to ask me about him always in the same terms "I say, old fellow, isn't there a fellow in your court called [Jimmy] Wigram?" – and upon my answering in the affirmative he rejoined, "Ah what a wild chap he was!" But he never told me, and of course I never asked, why.

James was universally recognised as a man of first-rate talent, with a most brilliant Cambridge reputation, which was fully sustained by his performances at the Bar. The highest honors were universally believed to be his due – and would in all probability have been attained by him but for a lamentable condition of heath. He was blessed with the sweetest temper I ever knew a man to possess – and which not only the wrangles of the

Court could never disturb, but which withstood the grievous torments of a teasing asthma – and the relentless inroads of a consumption which terminated his amiable and valuable existence at a comparatively early age. I don't think he was more than fifty years old.[5]

George Turner, a most excellent man, was in the Chambers next to mine in New Square – a model of hard work. I used to look up at his windows, on leaving at night, and rarely found his lamp extinguished. I found it was in vain that I did "out-watch the Bear." He was first Vice Chancellor and afterwords Lord Justice with Knight Bruce in the Court of Appeal. To me, he was always kind, friendly and encouraging.

Sutton Sharpe was in the foremost rank of rising men. He had more business and more pupils below the Bar than any other stuff gown – and after he took silk was on a fair way for promotion. He was a nephew of the poet Sam Rogers and was looked upon as his expectant heir. He was a constant visitor to Paris during the long vacation and had an extensive acquaintance among the French liberals and *littérateurs*. I passed several pleasant days with him in Paris, and through him was admitted, as a stranger to a *Cercle*, when I saw at dinner some of the celebrities, Émile de Girardin and several others, whose names I do not at this moment recollect. He took me once to dine (I suppose as M. Quatorze) with his aunt Miss Rogers, Sam Rogers's sister, where were present Miss Burdett (now Lady Burdett-Coutts), then young and handsome and fabulously rich. There were besides Monkton Milnes (Lord Houghton), [John] Bellenden Ker, John Romilly (later Lord Romilly), and several other prominent Whigs – but what I best remember was incessant mirth that was kept up by the ever-memorable Reverend Sydney Smith. Ker prated, tiresomely enough, about the rapid progress of civilization in the South Sea Islands. Besides education, which was spreading, their commerce, he said was flourishing; and they had a newspaper admirably conducted – with all the intelligence communicated by the ordinary European Press – price currents – the state of markets, etc., etc. "That is remarkable," said Smith. "Then I suppose you could see at a glance at what price you could buy a joint of cold clergyman." After the ladies had retired, the conversation turned naturally upon Miss Burdett and her enormous fortune

---

[5] Wigram in fact lived to age 73.

and her numerous aspirants. The Reverend, John in most urgent and affectionate terms, recommended Milnes not to miss the present opportunity of proposing to Miss Dives (as he called her), assuring him that Miss Rogers had kindly provided writing materials which were on her table in the next room. It was upon this occasion that in speaking of Macaulay, who had recently returned from India, he said he thought him greatly improved – "For now" he said, "there is occasionally a streak of silence in his discourse." It was altogether a pleasant afternoon, and I was intensely delighted at finding that all I had so frequently heard of the witty, kind, and genial priest did not surpass the reality. All poor Sharpe's brilliant expectations were fatally extinguished by an illness which attacked him suddenly – and to my sincere regret, and that of his numerous friends, he died of pleurisy, in his Chambers, which he had fitted up with taste and care as a residence at no small expense.

I cannot go through the long list of good men and dear friends with whom my lot was cast during the time I am referring to - Dear Pluslie, Kenyon Parker, John Walker, the Quaker, Selvyn, and many others – but they were almost all judges or eminent counsel, delightful companions and true friends and valuable help and made my existence thoroughly agreeable.

I must however spend a line or two upon a remarkable man who contributed to the general argument of our groups. This man, Dan Wakefield, who had been, as I was told, at one time in very considerable practice below the Bar – but who had for some unexplained reason outlived his popularity. He had lived a strange life of which I believe no one knew the particulars. He was of mature age when he had begun to practice at the Bar – but it appeared from his own statement that he had travelled and lived a good deal on the Continent of Europe. He said he had been a banker – a merchant – a member of the Irish Parliament before the Union – an agriculturist – and especially a famous breeder of sheep – and told marvelous stories about introducing Merino sheep into his farm in Essex. It was pleasant to listen to his account of having paid 300 guineas for a Merino ram in Northumberland, and bringing the animal with him in a post chaise to his Essex farm – and of his frequenting the Smithfield Market before daybreak on the Market days, because he could not trust the salesman. Whether he received it or not, he had acquired the reputation of being as great a liar as Fernando Mendes Pinto. Nobody believed a word he said, but he was universally listened to and generally liked. His lying was always amusing and never wicked or mischievous. It proceeded, I believe, merely from the warmth of his imagination – not fraudulent or impudent and vain like Bethell's. He was up to every trick upon the board, and some of his suggestions, of which he was not sparing, were often very useful to less experienced practitioners. I confess myself to be under obligations to him and his respect, and think that Lord Lyndhurst once paid him a well-deserved (left-handed) compliment when he said that Mr. Wakefield was "never deficient in resources." He was uncle or great uncle to a rascal whose abduction of a great heiress, a Miss Tanner, made a great noise. He died suddenly, quite an old man and was greatly missed if he was not greatly mourned.

It is not my intention, as I have said before, to give any detailed account of my doings in the Court of Chancery. They were not, in themselves, remarkable, nor different from the ordinary course of everyday business. Very interesting and to me very important while they were in action – but not worth relating. One of these industrious penny-a-liners, who are so busy nowadays in collecting memoirs which may feed the idle curiosity of what is called "the reading public" (Fitzroy) lately wrote to me announcing that he was collecting memoirs of men who had attained advanced ages and requested me to furnish him with materials relating to myself for his work. I answered him with King Lear: "'tis my intent to shake all cares and business from my age, conferring them to younger strengths, while I unburthened, crawl towards death."

Before, however, I part company with the Court of Chancery – for the present at least – I must mention one of its diversions which I look back upon with great pleasure. There had grown up a small society among the men most in business, who made a practice of dining at Greenwich once a year, just after the last meal and shortly before this commencement of the long vacation. No judges were admitted. With that exception, there was no rule but one viz., that the invitations to join should be unanimous. No black balls – but a shake of the head or a shrug of the shoulders amounted to a vote of exclusion. Wood (Lord Hathereley), then in full practice at the Bar, had been mentioned more than once – but although no one could say a word against him there seemed to be a notion among the others that he was not likely to add to the hilarity of the meetings – and when Spencer Walpole said he had nothing against him personally – and that he had no objection to go to church with him at any time or place, but that he would just as soon not dine with him at the Ship, the matter was settled. The society was in a sense aristocratic. Impudent and willful perhaps, but as its very spirit was that the members should be free from all control or censure – trusting one another implicitly – and not afraid to give free scope to their animal spirits and love of fun and not afraid to "play the fool" in a moderate degree they may be excused for being unwilling to admit any person who was notoriously wiser or better than themselves. And so, for once in the year, about a score of them dined together – not wisely but sometimes too well – and the ghost of Jo Mille, and songs and jokes, old and new, filled up the revels for many a merry hour, not forgetting that tobacco was not *au mauvais odeur*.

Home Life

In all this time my domestic life was most happy. It was not without its disappointments and its sorrows. The deaths of beloved relations and of most dear friends cast their dark shadows upon our existence. We endured the lot of mortality as well as time and a spirit of undying thankfulness, for we good that remained sustained us – and as it is my intention in this writing to adopt the motto of the sundial, and to chronicle of the hours. I decline to dwell upon them or to call up recollections which, although they can never be obliterated, it would be painful and useless here to recall.

As all that I have now to write is intended for not only indulgent eyes – but for those who are more or less intimately and personally acquainted with all that I can say, I shall briefly mention some of the events that concerned us all.

Our circumstances improved greatly. We thought we could afford a country house and a carriage. We had an admirable, fruitful, industrious servant, William Hanwell, whose good qualities entitled him to be farther considered as a true friend than as merely a servant. Our children grew up – the boys after being at the school of King's College went – two of them to Oxford. James, who was destined to be an attorney, was articled to Wetherell, who was at the head of one of the largest agency offices in London and was for several years my best and most valued client. Hugh was ordained, and became a curate to the Rector of St. George, Bloomsbury. Frank , after some months of pupilage with Dr. Greswell at Tortworth in Gloucestershire, went to Balliol, Oxford. Walter went to Eton. Sis, dearest Sis, my only daughter, remained under her mother's wing, and had all the advantages which could be derived from well selected instructors, with the inestimable value of the training and counsel and example of as wise and good and tender a parent as ever lived. The best praise I can bestow upon my children is to say that they were not insensible nor unworthy of the great advantages with which Providence had blessed them. Our first country house was Friern Watch at the north end of Finchley common − a roomy old fashioned house with a good garden and within 10 miles of London − a place that suited us admirably and which we occupied till about 1840 (as well as I recollect), when the landlord, having done some repairs which the house was greatly in want of − raised our rent (as we thought) unreasonable. I ought to have stated (and but that this chronicle has been written by fits and starts I should have done) of the before mentioned the country house that upon the expiration of our first year's lease in Coram Street in 1834 we took a better and larger house No. 36 in Upper Bedford Place, which we lived until the end of 1854.

Having quitted Friern Watch, we found a house at Willesden, which suited us very well and we dwelled there until 1849. I forget the reason that induced us then to change. I rather think it was the condition of the building. The landlord had not the means and I had not the inclination to make the necessary repairs. But however this was, we quitted Willesden and took a very quaint old-fashioned house at Mortlake. Of our several country houses, this was unquestionably the best. It was not in any sense attractive − externally or internally − but it had good commodious rooms and enough of them and a spacious garden which supplied us with fruit and flowers and kitchen vegetables. No prospect − but with numerous traditions relating to the reign of Charles I and the great tapestry manufacture in which it was said that the cartoons of Raphael were worked by the encouragement of that hapless monarch, by whose love of art and good taste those matchless productions were secured for England, and hard by – on the other side of the garden walls was a spacious old mansion said to have been occupied by [Henry] Ireton and often visited by [Oliver] Cromwell. The outer wall looked over the river and whether all that was said about its flourishing days was true or not it was sufficient to rouse the imagination and to dreams of times and men and things long passed away but not to be forgotten.

This residence had many advantages. Although I did not own an inch of land, I considered myself the owner in enjoyment (not the lord in title and possession) of three very grand properties: 1) The River Thames was as much mine as anybody else's. I could easily reach Richmond by water. 2) Kew was within easy reach by land or by water – and all its treasures were as much mine (or all purposes of enjoyment) as if I had been the owner of its magnificent trees and hot houses and museums. 3) Richmond Park, its broad lawns, beautiful plantations, its numerous troops of red deer, fallow deer, and nibbling flocks were mine whenever I chose to visit them – and all these wonders and delights were kept up for me, at enormous cost, the burden of which cost me no care.

All the leisure I could command – a every holiday (and they were more frequent then than they have become under the improved practice of the Court of Chancery) was fully employed and enjoyed in excursions and rambling while we lived at Mortlake – and I look back to that time with great pleasure. At a very easy distance from London – occasionally visited by dear friends – in pure air with agreeable occupations and recreations our days were passed in great enjoyment.

But our really great and thoroughly enjoyable holidays were the long vacations that the jealousy of the Common Law practitioners had long been directed against the advantages which the Equity Bar was supposed to enjoy. The restlessness of some attorneys who found or fancied that the course of justice was delayed because the time-honoured usage of shutting up the Temple of Themis for two or more months at that season of the year which, by common consent, in all professions and in many mere trades, had been devoted to comparative leisure and repose was denounced as a denial of justice. It is always easy to raise a cry – the press at this period was somewhat languid and with exhausted resources readily echoed the complaints at length, and the long vacation – if not abolished – was so hampered and curtailed that all its real enjoyments and, above all, its dependence were extinguished. It was not wholly destroyed, but it was miserably curtailed and disfigured. This is not the place for showing how merely vain and false and shortsighted were the reasons which found favor with the governing powers for establishing the changes that were adopted. If it were, I believe there would be no difficulty in demonstrating their utter worthlessness, and on soundness – but I do say that there never was a time when, or an occasion upon which, any complaint of wrong or any just assertion of right were precluded by reason of the Courts of Equity being closed for the hearing of causes in the vacation. The Lord Chancellor and the other judges were at all times accessible. Though some of them were absent sufficient numbers of others, and not difficult of access, were within reach. Enough of the offices for all reasonable purposes were open, and it is, in my opinion, wholly untrue that any injustice was done to the suitors because the months of September and October were not as much open daily as they were during the other months of the year.

It is useless and idle to deplore the mischiefs that were triumphant – and which can never be repaired. I prefer to look back upon some of the long vacations I have enjoyed – and to remind myself how pleasant such things were. I think that in the first or second year after our marriage, Mr. Giles, a stockbroker living at Enfield, lent us for a couple of months a small farm- house at Prince Stile, on the high ground between Tonbridge and Tunbridge Wells – a small and somewhat homely place but sufficient for all our wants and wishes. The country was very beautiful – the Medway, there but a small stream, lay at the foot of our hill. He rambled through the woods spent many long days in visiting Penshurst – the old mansion deserted – but containing remnants and memorials of its departed magnificence – filled with remembrances of Sir Philip Sidney – of his sister, "Pembroke's mother" and the noble personages and the noble deeds which there lived and were done in the great days afore time. We visited Sumner and renewed our acquaintance with recollections of the mirthful exploits of Grammont and his care-deriding crew. The "Wells" was within an easy walk (I could walk very well in those days). We tasted – I don't say we drank – the unpalatable, which were thought to be a panacea for "all the ills that flesh is heir to" and dreamed and thought upon the gay days.

Holidays and Travel

Before the next vacation came round, Mr. Giles had sold his little farmhouse, and we, being convinced that, for the health of the children and for other weighty reasons, a residence for some months in the country was desirable, took a small house at the western end of Enfield Town, which we inhabited for two months, perhaps more, during the vacation and until we took Friern Watch, which I have before mentioned. Nothing worth noticing happened to us during this period. We had pleasant long walks in a district not eminently picturesque but agreeable – though the New River in its peaceful sluggish course could not compare with the Medway in its infancy. We had a garden in which we took great interest – and a gardener, a humorous old rogue whose sayings and doings amused us. He had a consumptive daughter whom he maintained out of his scanty earnings – and although he did not grudge or complain, he did not scruple to consider this duty somewhat of a burden. "I've seed" he said, "the old birds feed and bring up their young – but I never seed the young birds feed the old uns." A former mistress of his, who had gone to settle in the West Indies, wrote to him desiring him to send her some garden seeds of which she enclosed him a long list, but she forgot to send him the money for them. However, being good natured, he made up a packet of such seed as he had and dispatched it. When it was suggested to him that the seeds would, upon growing, show that he had failed to comply with the lady's directions, he winked the only eye he had left and said "I was a thinking o' that and so I biled 'em." He brought us once a magnificent bloom of a snow-white rose – new then but which afterwards became common enough, and being asked its name he said "It's a funny name for its colour – it's called the Bould Nigger." "Oh, you must be mistaken," said somebody. "No, I'm not" said he "I read it in print in the nurseryman's catalogue." And there it was sure enough – *La Boule de Neige*. Though no scholar, he was a capital practical gardener full of contrivances and expedients and taught us many devices in grafting and budding and piping and other gardening conjuring.

But this memory of old Johnson has called me off from what I had intended to chronicle, viz.: the manner in which some of the long vacations were spent. It had become a firm conviction that, after the labours of the working year, it was indispensably necessary that I should take for some weeks a course of change. Change of scene and thought and occupation, and I believe that such a season of change and repose was in all respects wholesome and invigorating. In general, my dear wife, who worked as hard as I did, and stood as much in need of change as I did, accompanied me – and not only shared but enhanced all the benefit and all the enjoyment afforded by our trips.

The first of these but in which she was not my companion was a journey into Flanders and Holland in the year 1830. My good friend Benjamin Ball, one of the principal clerks in the then great commercial house of Jeremiah Harman (before the advent of the great Rothschild), had some mission to Amsterdam and invited me to accompany him, which I readily accepted. He was an accomplished linguist and well acquainted with foreign politics and literature. We crossed to Calais, where he found waiting for him one of the professional couriers often employed by the house of Harman for the transmission of despatches and valeurs to various places on the Continent. A very short time sufficed for instructing and dispatching the courier. His horse was brought to the door of the Hotel Dessin. His wife helped him to get into his portentous Jack Boots – and away he went to ride to [St.] Petersburg, a journey of about fourteen days! *Nous avons changé tout cela* – the courier's occupation's gone - and telegraphs and cables and the miracles of electricity have taught the world how to convey intelligence "from the Indus to the Pole" by easier and more rapid means. Ball and I pursued our journey through Flanders to Rotterdam by diligence and trek, stopping occasionally at Bruges, Ypres, Antwerp, and other towns and seeing the treasures which the churches and public buildings contained.

At Amsterdam, Ball had some business to transact, which led him to the Exchange, where I saw a multitude of merchants busily pursuing their traffic. At one o'clock, with great punctuality, all business was suspended. The gates were shut – the traders departed – and all of them went to the restaurants to dine. At 2 o'clock, the traffic was renewed – the merchants reassembled and for two hours, or more, the empire of commerce was resumed. Ball had letters of introduction to several of the most famous merchants, who had very fine collections of the great Low Country painters, and I saw there for the first time many masterpieces in that branch of art in which they excelled we found time to visit The Hague and came to the conclusion that no one can really feel and understand Rembrandt who has not looked upon him in this, his own country.

I had mentioned to Mr. Barnes my intended journey. The dispute between Holland and Belgium, which had been brewing for some time, had assumed an angry shape.[6] Barnes, who had always a very watchful eye to the interests of the *Times*, thought that something noteworthy might happen, and he requested me to take in Brussels on my way home and to let him know now matters were then proceeding. Ball was obliged to go straight home. So we parted company and I, nothing loathe, went on to Brussels. I found the city in a state of serious revolt. Many houses and shops shut up and barricaded. The National Guard was in arms, and detachments moving about – the whole population on the alert – great numbers of the citizens, not in uniform, but with cross belts over their ordinary clothes and with muskets upon their shoulders and keeping guard at various points. The only person I was acquainted with in Brussels was the Chevalier Hotton – an old *sabreur* of great fame in the old Napoleon's army. He was in the Moscow Campaign and used to tell the most moving stories about the disastrous retreat – and the dreadful Bridge of Berezina. The fingers of his left hand wounded by the front gave dismal token of part of his sufferings, but he was always in good spirits and indefatigably active. I had become acquainted with him at Woodbridge House and we were great friends. He was a comrade of Szliski and a crony of the little Count de La Garde. I went to look for him and was directed to a disused riding school in the lower part of the town. There I found him on horseback in a plain brown frock with his sabre belted on and no other distinction

---

[6] Bacon was witnessing the Belgian Revolution of 1830, which led to Belgium's national independence after an uneasy 15-year union with the Netherlands imposed after Napoleon's downfall.

than a crimson scarf. He was employed in drilling and directing an improvised troop of calvary – most of them young farmers from the surrounding country. All full of patriotic ardour – ready to fight – and despising the Dutch troops whom they were burning to encounter.

I learned from Hotton that war was inevitable and an attack upon the city was imminent. He had no misgivings as to the result and, although his hastily levied troops were raw, he was satisfied that they would give a good account of the more orderly and better trained enemy they were to meet. His drill being finished, and his troop dismissed, he gave me very full particulars of the actual state of affairs in Brussels – and took me to the Hôtel de Ville, where a committee of public safety was sitting *en permanence*, and introduced me to the president, whom I understood to be an eminent citizen and Magistrate. The *Times* was of course a name to conjure with, and the president, upon learning that I was corresponding with the paper, gave me all the particulars I required as to the state of affairs and several placards, addresses, and public documents. These I transmitted to Mr. Barnes with a long dispatch in which I gave him all the information I had been able to obtain and my own impressions respecting the condition and prospects of this city and its inhabitants. This task took up a good part of the evening – and having finished I was about to take my dispatch to the Post Office – but upon the landlord's suggestion that the streets were not safe for walking, especially for a stranger, I entrusted the parcel to his care and had the satisfaction of learning afterwards that it safely reached its destination in Printing House Square. I remained for some time in the front of the hotel, where several groups were assembled. All the town was astir; lampions blazing at the windows and some campfires at points of the pavements in the Montagne. The lower town was eliminated – smoke and confused noises filled the air. Patrols and mounted messengers traversed the streets. Soon after midnight, I went to bed and was fortunate enough to get to sleep after a very fatiguing day. On the following morning, having nothing further to learn or to do, nor any desire to take part in a quarrel which was none of mine, I departed for Paris – the road to which place was uninterrupted.

Some years after this I paid another visit to Brussels in company with my dear brother Henry. All was then quiet and flourishing. The Dutch

yoke had been thrown off – and the independence of the Kingdom of
Belgium firmly established. This however had not been accomplished
without some hard fighting, as we were told. A few days after my last visit,
the Dutch troops made serious attack upon the Faubourg and were repelled
by the Belgians who behaved with great gallantry and, although they
sustained heavy losses, they utterly defeated their foes. We heard many
stories, all, of course, to the honor and glory of the Belgians. The people
flocked to the scene of the fight *en masse* – peaceful citizens became
furious warriors. Even such of the clergy as were capable of bearing arms
were expected and often compelled to fall in and lend a hand in repelling
the invaders, and to fight under one banner *pro aris et focis*.

Among the servants of the church was a priest distinguished not
more for his corporal strength and good looks than for the exemplary
discharge of his spiritual duties. He was looked upon as a Son of the
Church. All this did not exempt him from the necessity of bearing arms.
He was enrolled – furnished with a musket and bayonet and a cartouche
box – and in a famous sortie from the rampart he made such good use of
his unfamiliar weapons that he was seen to dispatch two of the Dutch
soldiers and to do other deeds of valour which drew upon him universal
admiration. His prowess in arms and his good fortune were so remarkable
that he became a sort of popular hero. But after the pacification, and when
the fervour of the citizens had somewhat cooled, doubts began to be
entertained about the inevitable consequence which must ensue from his
deeds of the arms having regard to his holy calling. There may have been
well grounded objections to his resuming his ministration – there may have
been some degree of envy among his less distinguished clerical brethren.
However this may have been, he was summoned before an ecclesiastical
tribunal which, after due deliberation, came to the conclusion that while
his hands might be said to be yet red with the blood of his fellow creatures,
he was unfit to discharge the sacred duties of his profession, and he was
accordingly sentenced to be suspended from his office.

This judgment, ruinous to the poor young priest, was highly
unsatisfactory to many of the citizens as well as those who admired his
valour as those who esteemed his private character. Meetings were held
and an appeal to the Pope was determined – but as this would take some

time and would be attended with considerable expense, a subscription was raised and very generously contributed to – and the priest found himself in possession of more money than he had ever before owned. Then it was that the Spirit of Evil tempted him. Brussels was, and I believe it still is, famous as a beer-drinking town. Large, spacious open restaurants are numerous and highly attractive. The priest, greatly dissatisfied at the treatment he had received, bethought himself that his mother Church had proved herself a harsh and, as he thought, an unjust stepmother to him, so he laid out a good part of the subscription in the purchase of a famous beer shop, whereby the help of many gaslights, and not a little by the attraction of showy, blonde Rubens-like barmaids he soon established a roaring trade in Boks of Louvain, Faro, Zelsan, and other products of John Barleycorn.[7] *Il jettait son froc aux orties* and settled down as a thriving victualer.

I made several other long vacation trips, the general recollection of which is often a source of great pleasure. I did not keep any journal, but I wrote often and most fully to my wife. It is possible that some of my letters may yet remain in a forgotten corner, and if there be any such, they will tell better than I can remember of the places I visited and the impressions I received. Once I joined Joe Parker and his wife in a visit to Venice – an enchanted place – full of ghosts, Titian, Bellini, Tintoretto, Shylock, Voltaire, Goldoni, Byron, and a multitude of other disembodied spirits.

Once I visited La Grande Chartreuse, a gloomy, soul-saddening monument of human superstition. A much more agreeable visit was made with J. Arden and his wife to the South of France – Marseilles, Asme, Arles, Avignon, Vaucluse, and returning to Paris we passed through the Cévennes – the scene of the cruel *dragonnades* under Louis XIV and Marshal Villars, and of Alexandre Dumas's charming memoir which, if it is not all true, might or ought to be. (My recollection of the Cévennes has been lately refreshed by a book of [Matilda] Betham-Edwards called *The Roof of France*, which does the subject very little justice).

---

[7] John Barleycorn, the subject of an English folksong, is the personification of barley and its alcoholic products, whiskey and beer.

Further Recollections

March 1890

I really do not know why I should occupy myself – and tire my readers (if I should have any) with all this rigmarole of narratives, which however they may interest me, cannot have any power to move them. But as I have nothing other or better to do, I must go on for a while to conjure up the recollections (as well as I can), of times and scenes and events in which I was engaged. I find myself with nothing to do. My life, once a very active one, has become painfully dull – I have drifted, from a flowing stream and bright skies, into a sluggish, if not stagnant, backwater – with a foggy atmosphere all around and about me. The scribbling at least makes me forget for a time the change that has come over me, so on I go and forget what I am by remembering what has been.

My wife was as willing as I was to diversify our life by occasional trips abroad. We visited France several times. One journey (I forget the year) was spent in Normandy. We crossed from New Haven and spent about three weeks visiting the famous old cities and their magnificent and romantic Cathedrals. I was then somewhat bitten with antiquarian propensities. (It was in the reign of Walter Scott and the disease was prevalent). Rouen, Caen, Lisieux, Coutances – the view of Jersey from the tower of the Cathedral, the Seine with castles on its banks – Tancarville, the ruins of Jumièges, Poussin's birthplace at Les Andalys, Château Gaillard, and orchards of the cider-drinking population. The memories of the Black Prince, of Henry V, and the heroes of Shakespeare's historical plays, not forgetting the noble and ill-fated Joan of Arc – gave an interest of ever present force at every step – and would lean me into *longueurs* which I must not indulge myself, or tire my readers with dilating upon.

At Christmas, we passed a very merry holiday at Rickmansworth, when Mr. and Mrs. Arden held a sort of housewarming, and where dancing and private theatricals and other diversions kept a large company in full play for several days. The younger ones, mad with fun and good spirits, and the elder, hardly less joyous though they were sorry that they were no longer younger.

In the following year (1840) we went to Boulogne and in a subsequent year, the exact date or which I do not remember, where we passed the whole of the vacation. We had a patient – not brilliant – tutor for the boys (a Mr. Jones) and dancing and other branches of education were seriously cultivated. Sea bathing and trips into the surrounding country, which though it is not picturesque, very agreeably diversified our amusements, and we came back in good health and spirits – and knowing at least a little more of French "as it is spoken" than we did before. During our stay, King Louis-Philippe paid a visit to Boulogne, and we had the satisfaction of hearing him make a speech in the marketplace to the soldiers of the National Guard, whom he called *"Messieurs les camarades"* – they being under arms and he in uniform.

My dear wife and I made a little jaunt of our own while we were at Boulogne. We hired a small shandrydan drawn by a steady horse well known to and highly respected by the visitors, rejoicing in the name of Grey Momus. We went along the coast towards the Lille – visited Dunkirk, saw the ruined Abbey of St. Bertin at Douai, Arras, the great tapestry school where Raphael is said to have been worked; the field of the Cloth of Gold – Ardres – St. Pol and some other towns of interest – and enjoyed a week's holiday to ourselves, free from domestic troubles. Oh happy days!

This was soon after the foolish, fruitless escapade of Louis-Napoleon [Bonaparte] and his tame eagle.[8] The towns upon the coast contained several detachments of troops which had been sent to check, if necessary, the proposed invasion (for it seems that, through the folly or the perfidy of some of Louis-Napoleon's adherents, all his movements were well known to the French government) and we were warned that it might be inconvenient to us if we should meet any of the French soldiery. *La perfide Albion* was suspected of favoring Louis-Napoleon's attempt. We found at Douai some regiments quartered there. We accordingly held a council of war and soon came to the determination that French officers

---

[8] Napoleon's nephew, Louis-Napoleon Bonaparte, was the heir to his legacy and attempted an uprising after landing in France in August 1840. Quickly apprehended, he was sentenced to life in prison but in 1846 he escaped and returned to France after Louis-Philippe abdicated in February 1848. Later that year, Napoleon was elected France's president. In 1852, successfully staged a coup to make himself Emperor.

must be more or less gentlemen – and believing that harmless travelers of such an appearance as we presented could not excite suspicion, we agreed to risk the danger if there were any. This landlord upon our suggesting that we should like some dinner congratulated us for that he had a *table d'hôte* much better than ordinary because some of the officers of the regiment and some of the landowners of the district were to be his guests. And so we found it. There were perhaps a dozen officers. The commandant received us very politely – seated Madame in the place of honour at table – and all went on with admirable good-breeding. The conversation was cheerful and not an allusion to politics. The weather was warm. The commandant said it reminded him of some days he had passed at Rouen shortly before, where his duty had called him to check an expected event of the workmen in that city, and where he said he had been very civilly entertained by the authorities. His reception took place in the Episcopal Palace, and he was chatting before dinner with the Archbishop – the heat of the weather being naturally the topic, the officer said he had suffered throughout the day from excessive thirst upon which the Archbishop called up to him a short fat bald-headed priest – a dignitary no doubt – and told him what the officer had been saying and commanded him especially to the care of the " round fat oily man of God" and then turning to the officer he said *"Monsieur le commandant, nous vous chargeons de vous altérer."* And the soldier said His Eminence kept his word for he was supplied abundantly with as good wine as he ever drank.

On the following day we pursued our journey and got comfortably back to Boulogne after a little trip which I look back upon with great pleasure. We made many other very agreeable trips all worthy of remembrance, but I am sorry to say that for want of any written note or record I am quite unable to state with any approach to accuracy the places and the events which ought to be the most interesting in the narrative that I ought to give. I have asked dear Sis, whose memory is more retentive than mine and whose impressions must be fresher, to help me. If she should keep her promise and I should find time to avail myself of her assistance, I will fill up as well as I may the blank which I am compelled to leave in my chronicle. [Updated April 1890] Sis, has, since I wrote the preceding paragraph, given me the notes I have asked her for, and I have compiled the story of our foreign adventures. I think it more convenient that I should keep it apart from my general history. I intend therefore to make up an appendix that will not interfere with this narrative.

It was at the end of 1853 that we transferred ourselves from Bedford Place to No. 1, Kensington Garden Terrace. I cannot say that I quitted our former residence without regret. We had been upon the whole fortunate, and although, as was unavoidable sorrows and disappointments had occasionally fallen upon us, hope and necessity were ever present. For active exertion, had enabled us to bear present and unavoidable griefs and encouraged us to believe that the future would not be less favorable than the better part of the past had been. My Guardian Angel, my dear wife, had a conviction that we should do better by removing westward. My reliance upon her clear judgment and never-failing good sense induced me readily to adopt her views. We examined many "houses to let," discussed with great patience and care their several advantages, and at length, in what I may call a happy moment, we determined to take the house which I thence forward and to the present time have occupied. It cost us the larger part of all that we then possessed, but I believe that our money was employed with great judgment thanks to her determination and to the advantages of all concerned. For the best part of 40 years, we have lived in a commodious, comfortable house, free from the carking cares of having to pay rent on Quarter Day – an intolerable slavery!

By this time, somewhat serious thoughts about the future began occasionally to occupy my mind. The uncertainty of all human affairs, especially those connected with them ever-changing condition of my profession – and the fact that I had a growing family whose position and future prospects were necessarily dependent upon my position often occasioned me moments of uneasiness. My boys were growing up, Hugh having graduated at Oxford had determined to take Holy Orders. James was destined to be a solicitor. Walter was to go to Eton – and Sis was pursuing her studies at home. All seemed to be tranquil. By the admirable management of my dear wife our expenses were so conducted that every year more than sufficed not only for our desires but so as to make considerable (for us) accumulations to the property we had acquired, without curtailing the enjoyments which we permitted ourselves. Hugh got a curacy, first in Queen's Square in the church in which my father and mother were married. By the kindness and generosity of dear John Romilly – (perhaps mainly by the never to forgotten thoughtful regard born to us by his most dear wife) James, who had been articled to a solicitor, was appointed to a good post in the office of the Master of the Rolls, which established him for life. Lord Cranworth as Chancellor had the clerical patronage appurtenant to his office and upon my application to him he presented Hugh to the living of Baxterley (Warwickshire), worth 2 to 3 hundred pounds a year. Two of the boys were thus so far provided for. Frank was in a fair way of attaining his place at the Bar, and dear Walter was a promising boy. All apparently of sound constitutions – well-grown – in good health and good spirits – and we were all filled with joy and hope and grateful, I hope, for all God's goodness to us.

Griefs and the Loss of Laura

From 1854 to 1859 we were greatly satisfied and pleased with our new house and all went on with great smoothness upon the whole. I have already said it is not my intention to dwell upon the details of our domestic life, and it is the less necessary that I should do so since the only persons for whose perusal these notes are intended know them all quite well and recollect them much better than I can. All that was grievous and painful – and of course we were not without our sorrows and disappointments (which I would rather not recollect) while I am most grateful for the happiness I enjoyed. One sad and memorable loss we sustained in the death of our dear boy James.

He was apparently in perfect health until he was attacked by a pulmonary complaint which soon presented alarming symptoms. Romilly granted him the necessary leave of absence and Hugh accompanied him to Italy, where after only a few weeks he sank under the fell complaint. It was intended that he should return, but his strength so completely failed that he could proceed no further than Lyons, where his brother followed him to the foreign grave in which he was buried. We afterwards visited the cemetery where he had caused a memorial to be placed, and shed our unavailing tears over the spot which contained his remains. "Whom the Gods love die younger." Our only consolation was the recollection of his blameless life, and to our grief was the belief that had his life had been spared he would have been deservedly our pride as well as our joy.

But a heavier sorrow was at hand! My ever dear wife had complained of ailments which disturbed her health, generally so good that we regarded them without anything like alarm. In the spring of 1859, she for the first time during our married life was compelled to call for medical assistance. Up to that time she had suffered nothing but the most ordinary inconveniences and had never kept to her bedroom and had always readily regained her usual hearty cheerful good spirits and was a lasting joy to all who surrounded her. There is too much reason to believe that her active exertions in saving (as she did) the life of her mother in a very serious illness, and during a winter of unusual severity, so impaired her strength that she never thoroughly regained it. She was at that time not 20 years old. Immediately on her mother's recovery, she was assailed by an attack of rheumatic Fever and lay for many days in the most imminent danger, and though she recovered and was thenceforward full of vigour and health, the injury she suffered was never repaired.

We had the help of a very able medical man, Mr. Field, a general practitioner and our near neighbor, who had at first appeared to think that there was nothing serious in the nature of the attack and who promised, and no doubt believed, that a few days would restore his patient, but when, finding that she could not leave her bedroom, he became more anxious and recommended us to call in the assistance of Sir Henry Watson. The physician came and for some days all seemed to be proceeding safely when quite suddenly symptoms of the most alarming kind appeared. It is not possible to express the dismay which seized us all – the shock we felt on receiving the fatal intelligence that no hope of recovery remained. I have preserved a note written immediately after this most crushing misery and well it is that I did so, for I could not trust myself to write about it again.

Wednesday the 30th of March 1859. Fatal day! On coming home at four o'clock, Mr. Field met me – and told me that Laura was very ill. His manner filled me with alarm. Dr. Watson had been, and I was told was of the opinion that she was worse than when he had seen her the day before. In short, without recollecting exactly what he said, he convinced me that there was no hope. All depended, he said, upon her taking sufficient nourishment to excite and sustain the action of the heart, which was so feeble that her pulse was hardly perceptible. I went up to her room – they were raising her in bed for the purpose of swallowing some cold beef tea with brandy. She was labouring under great difficulty of breathing than she had been before. She was supported while she took readily, even eagerly, the drink. She saw and recognized me – then, alas, for the last time – said "You are here" – desired Eliza with some indistinctness of utterance to arrange her pillows. This being done she sank back and fell into a sort of slumber, muttering occasionally words of prayer of which all that I could catch were "Father in Heaven" and "heavenly grace." She occasionally opened and fixed her eyes, but for a moment only, and then closed them. Her lips moved, sometimes, as I fear, with an expression of pain. I stood by her bedside and with sister gave her every three quarters of an hour a small quantity of beef tea and brandy, which she took through a tube. I am sure she knew that we were with her, although a heavy languor and slumber prevailed. Her hands – the left hand chiefly became very cold, and one or other of us continued to chafe and warm it. Eliza and sister rubbed her feet, which though not very warm were not remarkably cold. Mr. Field entreated, insisted upon my going downstairs – dinner being served – and attempted to eat. I went down for ten minutes, and then returned to the bedside and sent down Sister, who took some nourishment. We then remained in the bedroom. From what Mr. Field had said, I thought the night would be very distressing and had arranged that Eliza should go to bed and sleep till 12 o'clock, when I intended that Sister should go to bed. Sister, Frank, Walter, and I remained in the room. After some time, I sat down, and, believing that I should have to watch through the night, I tried and after some time did go to sleep.

I know not how long I slept, but about 8 o'clock I woke up and approached the bed. Frank had her hand in his. Sister was endeavouring to get her to take some beef tea. Her position was just the same as it had been since between 4 and 5 o'clock – lying on her right side, her right hand under her cheek. All of a sudden, I perceived that the laborious breathing which had heaved the bed clothes at every respiration had ceased. So calm did she appear that I thought she was breathing more quietly. Alas! She had ceased to breathe. She had died – passed away without gasp or struggle or the slightest movement that could indicate that she was no more. In our alarm and doubt, Mr. Field was sent for and came immediately. It was no longer doubtful. She had departed from us, and amidst the bitter unavailing grief that filled our hearts our only consolation was that her dissolution had been without pain. The best and truest heart had ceased to beat. Her divine spirit had fled in full trust in the mercy of God, and we were left to weep a loss which nothing can ever supply.

Thursday and the other days till Monday were passed by us in deep misery. The kind condolences of friends – the sincere sorrow which they all expressed for our loss – and for their own – of that kind, genial, bright spirit which made joy and sunshine whenever she appeared, were all so many consolations to us, to know that she was loved as she deserved to be by all who knew her, is something.

Hugh and his wife came to London and Annie offered to stay with Sister. I am afraid I must have been thought ungrateful, but the sight of a strange face seemed an intrusion on our sorrows, and they stay with us only until the last sad affair is over.

Fanny came immediately and has done for us all that a tender loving spirit can do.

Monday, the 4th of April, we followed the remains of all that was dearest to me on earth to their last resting place in Paddington Cemetery. In a grave barely opposite to the entrance of the Chapel, westward we laid her and returned with broken hearts to the now desolate home which she had made the abode of joy and love. Joy departed forever! Love now drowned in bitter sorrow.

Since I write this for a memorial, let me not omit the manner in which my children have behaved. They are her children, reared and brought up by her, fostered with her precepts. Strengthened and formed after her example and worthily have they shown themselves. Active, affectionate, hiding their own griefs for the purpose of assuaging mine. They have done everything that I could have wished or hoped – everything that she could have desired. God (whose mercy has been shown to us for many years) – and may His grace be continued to us – knows what is best and we must, however sorrowing, to his will. Perhaps it is one of His mercies that she should have first departed. She is at least spared the agonies I now endure. She sleeps the sleep of the just. The world's troubles can reach her no more, and in the hope of a joyful resurrection – a reunion in that better existence which the revelation of God has promised us through his son Jesus Christ we have buries all that was mortal of her. In our hearts will live as long as they beat the recollection of her virtues – the tender remembrance of that love which was all that gladdened my existence.

I can write no more – the pen would fall from my hand if I made the attempt. More than thirty years have passed since my broken heart began to bleed at my irreparable loss, and it bleeds still as I read over the note I wrote while I was in deep agony.

K. G. T. 19th April 1890

Thoughts on World Affairs

Brighton, 31 December 1870

A year to look back upon. In the latter half of that year the French Empire has crumbled away. Its renowned army has been defeated and many thousands of its warriors carried into captivity.[9] Its strongest frontier fortresses taken, its glories extinguished. The Emperor [Napoleon III] a willing prisoner at [Wilhelmshöhe Castle, in Germany], his wife in exile, his son disinherited, Paris invested and, as would seem, on the point of being taken, the country wasted, the bravest of its defenders slain or captured. Desolate homes, misery in its worst forms weighing heavily on the people, levies hastily made and badly led, a government, such as it is, made up of a few inconsiderable persons without any reasonable probability of its being able to escape from certain defeat. A more miserable story of the past, a more saddening prospect of the future cannot be conceived.

And we are not without well grounded apprehensions that woe may be about to visit us. In Europe, a too evident desire on the part of Germany to quarrel, Russia threatening to break that treaty upon which the

[9] Bacon writes of the Franco-Prussian War of 1870-1871, which saw the defeat of the French Second Empire, the fall of Napoleon III, and the consolidation of Germany as united nation-state under Prussia's leadership.

peace and security of the world depends, America insolent, exacting, and hostile now pressing, and now withholding *Alabama* Claims[10] and ready and well disposed to pick a quarrel about fishery rights, and any other pretext upon which a dispute may be fastened. Ireland, supposed to be pacified by the concessions on the Church Establishment and the land questions, now avows an open intention to rebel unless independence of government and equal national rights are conceded.[11] It is in vain to think that we have done all that justice requires, that we have made even greater sacrifices, and practice a self-restraint which goes to the very edge, if it does not overpass all that a due regard for our national dignity (which is only another word for national independence and security) required or permitted. If it must be that we shall be forced into a war, the only satisfactory reflection is that we have done nothing to provoke it – that we have done much to prevent it – and the rest must be left to fate.

It is the duty of all men, the habit of most men, having arrived at an advanced period of life, to look back upon the years they have passed through and to endeavor to draw from the retrospect a distinct perception of the true nature and effect and the just proportions of the events in which they have been actors – and to ascertain with as much accuracy as, in the mist of self-love, they are capable of exercising in what they have satisfied their more mature judgments, and in what respects their natural and personal infirmities have misled them.

In that condition do I find myself at this moment. More than ten years have elapsed since, somewhat tired of constant and burdensome exertions, with diminished physical strength and an ability of that degree of animal spirits which had made me mock at toil, an opportunity presented itself of retiring from very onerous exertions – and (hope told a flattering tale) of passing so much as might be left to me of life in comparative quiet.

---

[10] *Alabama* Claims were U.S. demands for compensation from the U.K. for damages caused during the American Civil War by Confederate ships built in British shipyards. The main vessel involved was the *CSS Alabama*, which captured some 60 Union vessels before being sunk in the English Channel in 1864. The claims were settled by international arbitration in 1872, with Britain required to pay $15.5 million to resolve the dispute. The process is regarded as the founding case of international arbitration.
[11] Ireland's status remained unresolved until 1922, with questions remaining thereafter and down to the present day.

The Court of Bankruptcy

Lord Chancellor Cairns (See Appendix A) proposed to me [in 1868] to become a Commissioner of Bankruptcy. I had for many years been conversant with the law and practice in bankruptcy – I thought I knew it from its beginning to its end – its ins and its outs all the tricks and devices by which dishonest debtors sought to shift the loads from their own backs to those of their creditors – and by which eager and unscrupulous creditors tried to get the better of others who had been induced to trust the debtors – and of the unwholesome brood of legal practitioners and other unclean animals (scenting the carcass) bent upon sharing in the spoils – and practicing upon the *corpus vile* the most revolting experiments.

Therefore, nothing loathe, I accepted thankfully the Lord Chancellor's offer and thereupon took my place as Commissioner of Bankruptcy on 7 September 1868. I succeeded a very good-tempered, genial man, whose death had occasioned the vacancy which I (unworthily) filled. I don't think, to do him justice, that he ever thought or affected to think, that he possessed any knowledge of the law – but he was a man of good sense – [he] had an innate love of justice, a scorn of chicanery, and a deep disgust for these slippery and dirty practices which he was doomed, more or less, to become acquainted with. My colleagues, if I might respectfully call them by that name, were Holroyd and Winslow. The first was a thoroughbred special pleader, the son of a judge who had won his place on the bench by force of his well earned reputation in mysterious and then highly honored science called Special Pleading – a science, the great merit of which was to divert the attention of the courts to which questions of right and just between the parties litigant could be diverted and forwarded from the side of right by the subtle ingenuity. It might rather be called dexterity, by which the real points in issue could be diverted by the cunning and chicanery of practitioners. But my Holroyd who had sought a refuge from the manufacturer of demurrers – and pleas – and rejoinders and rebutters and surrebutters in the sacred precincts of Basinghall Street – relinquished readily his carefully acquired common law lore and dealt with the cases before him, as well as he could understand them, without special pleading tricks, but without the slightest knowledge or understanding of the enlarged principles of equity by which the

Bankruptcy Law had been administered by Lord Hardwicke and Lord Eldon in whom the supreme authority on bankruptcy was then vested and who were guided by principles of equity properly so-called, and which when understood form the quintessence of judicial determination.

My other colleague was Winslow, who had been several years a clerk in the department. Extremely assiduous and diligent in the discharge of his duties, in all points a respectable and worthy man who had found favor with Bethell – but as I know that the places in the Court of Bankruptcy were at that time the subjects of sale and barter between the aspirants to places and Dick Bethell, who had at that time great influence with his father, I am hardly at liberty to suppose that it was from a conviction of his ability and fitness and with a view to the public benefit Bethell, Lord Chancellor, selected Mr. Winslow from numerous barristers, men of standing, eminence, and worth to fill the place. However, he was appointed by Bethell to be a commissioner. He discharged the duties of the office most satisfactorily, and when the offices were abolished received the grant of a pension to the full amount of his salary, £2000 a year for the term of his natural life.

I continued in my post of Commissioner of Bankruptcy until the end of 1869, when Lord Hatherley's new Bankruptcy Act came into operation. Then I became, as afterwards stated, Chief Judge in Bankruptcy and so continued until after I was appointed Vice Chancellor. I cannot say that this period of my life was very pleasant or satisfactory. My decisions were very frequently reversed by the Lords Justice [William] James and [George] Mellish. I am not vain enough to think that I was in all cases right, but I am quite certain that they were often flagrantly wrong. My dear friend, James the Fat, was a true Welshman and was possessed by that evil and vindictive spirit which characterizes his countrymen. In former days, I am afraid that I had given him proof that I did not hold him in the highest estimation and I may have trodden on his corns – as did also Sutton Sharpe and John Romilly and others of mutual friends. His turn had come. Mellish, and admirable common lawyer, knew absolutely nothing of the law in bankruptcy – one of the main features of which consisted of the equitable principles which Lord Eldon and other eminent judges in Chancery from Lord Hardwicke downwards had now conclusively

adopted as established – and Mellish being very ill, readily surrendered to
James. He, I verily believe (without meaning to be spiteful) could not resist
the temptation of paying me off, and as few cases in bankruptcy could
afford an appeal to the House of Lords, he had his triumph. Howe did not
use me worse than he did Romilly, whose life he embittered if he did not
shorten it.

Vice Chancellorship

What has my year been? At the beginning, I found myself Chief Justice in
Bankruptcy very much against the intention and wishes of my old friend
the Lord Chancellor. The new system which differed more in name and
form than in substance from the old one went on smoothly enough on the
whole. The Registrars and other officers I believe were willing to do all
they could to make the administration effectual – and for all I know it has
done as well as could be expected in town and country. It very soon
became apparent that the office of Chief Justice was not an onerous one.
Appeals from the county courts were of very rare occurrence, and while
[Richard] Selwyn and [George] Giffard (dear friends ever to be lamented,
and whose loss, to me, can never be supplied) were Lords Justice the
appeals to the Superior Court were dealt with in a very satisfactory
manner. Selwyn, indeed, died before the new system came into operation.
Giffard, unlike some of his predecessors, did not think it expedient to
baffle the plain justice of cases and the plain meaning of the statutes for
the purpose of showing his own acuteness or perseverance, and under such
supervision the faults of the new system would not have produced any
public inconvenience. Alas, this was not to last. That malady under which
Giffard had been suffering for years renewed its attacks and after some
weeks of great suffering all our hopes of his recovery (which had been
sanguine) were extinguished. The world lost an upright, high-minded
judge, of the highest ability in his profession, and we lost a dear friend,
whose worth had made him universally beloved.

Then the Lord Chancellor was embarrassed. He had long revolved
in his lofty mind a scheme for remodeling the whole judicial system. He
had prepared a bill founded in some degree upon the Report of the
Judicature Commission, but, as I believe, the work of his own hands. He

brought it into the House of Lords without the slightest consultation or communication with any of the judges either of Law or Equity – a course wholly inexplicable – as much opposed the precedent and reason as it was deficient in the commonest courtesy. Well, it did not go so smoothly as he had expected – perhaps he was misled by the easy triumph he had enjoyed in the passing of the Irish Acts. He was compelled wholly against his will to appoint a Lord Justice in the place of Giffard, and so he selected James. This occasioned a vacancy in the office of Vice Chancellor, and then I was appointed to that office.

I should be very sorry if I thought I was deficient in any feelings of gratitude which I ought to entertain to the Lord Chancellor. But my firm conviction is that I owe him nothing on this score. When the Bankruptcy Bill was passing in the House of Commons in the summer of last year, I am certain that he intended to destroy the office which I then held and that he intended to appoint [George] Bramwell, or some other common law judge to the Chief Justiceship in Bankruptcy.[12] The common law judges are all very desirous of escaping from the cost and toil of going circuit and the painful work at the Old Bailey, and notwithstanding standing Branwell's protestation to me that he would not have accepted the office, and notwithstanding the Lord Chancellor's resolute silence on the subject, I am convinced, for reasons which it would be tedious here to set down, that this was the scheme.

Some of the men in the House of Commons seemed to have thought that the Chancellor's scheme was absurd and they so plainly expressed their opinions that the project was dropped. Palmer expressed himself plainly and with more than his usual warmth on the subject, and several other members spoke to me by name as to the fit person to place at the head of the New Bankruptcy Court – and as I understand made the matter so plain to [Prime Minister William] Gladstone that he was compelled to give in. I have no reason to think that the Lord Chancellor had been more communicative to him than to other persons on the subject of his little plan. However this may have been, Jessel told me that after the

---

[12] In fact no such thing happened. Bacon remained Chief Bankruptcy Judge concurrently with his new post as Vice Chancellor until 1883, when the bankruptcy post was transferred to the Queen's Bench division of the High Court of Justice.

matter had been discussed he said to [Lord Chancellor Roundell] Palmer "you ought to explain the matter to Gladstone who does not seem to understand it." Palmer, who, I suppose, was not in a mood to approach Gladstone in any other than a hostile attitude declined to do so. Therefore Jessel spoke to Gladstone himself and told him what he had to say about me, which was flattering, told him that he did not think I cared about any increase of salary but that I should be – and others would be displeased at my being passed over – that the public service would be supplied by my being appointed Chief Justice – and that he had no doubt I would accept it provided it was understood that upon a vacancy happening among the common law judges or the Vice Chancellors I should be appointed. To this Jessel told me Gladstone acceded and so in fact I was appointed Chief Justice by the House of Commons and certainly not by the Lord Chancellor.

I have not the least reason to doubt the exactness of Jessel's narrative of what took place between himself and Gladstone. Nay more, although Palmer has never spoken to me on the subject, I believe he has stated something to the like effect to other persons. Whenever I have met the Lord Chancellor he has evinced the same friendliness of manner as has been usual between us for forty years past, but I think he knows in his heart that he meant to do me an ill turn. And of very ill turn he would have done me if he had had his own way, for it was out of the question that this saving government would have given me a pension for the loss of my office or Commissioner – I could not have asked for it, having been only a few months in the post, and I should have been condemned to a life of obscurity and inaction for so much of it as may remain. However, this evil has been escaped.

After the Lord Chancellor had for a long while withstood the attacks upon him in the newspapers and elsewhere for not appointing a Lord Justice after Giffard's death, he was driven to fill up the place. By what considerations he was moved to appoint James Lord Justice I cannot guess. I do not believe it was for any love he bears him or any confidence he has in him. But so it was. I met him one morning in July in Lincoln's Inn Fields, and he stopped to shake hands and so forth. In the course of the same day, I received a note from him offering me the Vice Chancellorship and saying he had longed to tell me of it when we had met in the morning but was not then sure that James had accepted the Lord Justiceship. Now notwithstanding that I think I have a good deal to complain of in the Lord Chancellor, I must injustice to him express my belief that all he has done or omitted has been without any dislike of or intentional unkindness to me. He fixes his mind upon some object to be accomplished. He persuades himself that he is discharging a duty – and this conviction once attained I believe he would hang his own father without scruple and rejoice that he had acted according to the dictates of his conscience. I entered upon my new office of Vice Chancellor on 2 July 1870 and continued, sitting on the Mondays in Bankruptcy, till the beginning of the long vacation.

Another Grief

At this time, my poor Walter had assumed a very alarming form. I went to Malvern as soon as I could leave London and found him in such a condition as precluded all hope of his ultimate recovery. He had rallied from the last attack but was still deplorably ill, and although the doctors said that there was reason to believe that he might be restored, I was convinced that there was no chance of his overcoming the malady. Ellen had fitted up a bed for him in the drawing room – and by the effect of her care and the remedies which were applied he got so much better as to be able to get up daily, and at length to go upstairs to his usual bedroom. After staying several days at Malvern, I went back to Compton and stayed there until I was summoned again to Malvern, a change for the worse having taken place. I found Walter much weaker, and plainly convinced that there was no possibility of his recovery. From this time his strength gradually declined until on the last day of September just at daybreak he expired. For several days before, I think he had been unconscious, he was wholly without pain, and died without pang. Poor, dear boy – my friend and companion whose cheerful mirth and gay spirits had enlivened many a dull hour of my existence. Thoughtful and kind not only to me, but to everybody about him, in his last moments thinking kindly and providently and charitably for all resigned and pious, leaving us not without deep regret- but with sincere resignation to the Divine Will. A loss not to be supplied in this world – and the only consolation for which is the hope and belief that in another state of existence we may be reunited. In the quiet churchyard of Malvern Wells I followed him to the grave and shed bitter tears over his too early death.

How can I thank my dear Ellen and her kind husband for the affectionate care with which they had tended him during his long illness? For many days and nights, Sis and Ellen had never left his room. Hopkinson had daily prayed with his and administered to him religious consolation which soothed his mind and prepared him for that better existence which I doubt not he is now enjoying.

With depressed spirits I went back to Compton. Dear Frank was obliged to go to London to attend his revising. Hugh and Annie remained with me for some time. The revising finished, Frank came back and we all returned to London at the end of October. Then the work of the term was renewed, and things went on in their dull routine to the end of the year.

At Christmas, Frank and I went to Brighton. After staying there a week, Frank was called to London for a special examination. I stayed a day or two longer – the weather was excessively severe and I got very tired of being alone and so came home. And thus ends the year 1870, which has been full of care and anxiety and grief, mixed with a certain share of prosperity, and for the good and the evil, both of which are no doubt the dispensations of infinite wisdom. I pray to God that I may be thankful as I ought to be.

Knighthood

Saturday, 14 January 1871, I was summoned by the Secretary of State for the Home Department to present myself at Osborne for the purpose of being knighted.

Upon my appointment as Chief Judge, the Lord Chancellor had intimated to me that Mr. Gladstone – and he thought also – that I undergo this ceremony. In answering his letter, I expressed my unwillingness to assume the title, which was neither necessary to the office nor consistent with such a position and above all with such a salary as, in their generosity, the government had thought fit to assign to the office. And I so prevailed upon the Lord Chancellor that I heard nothing more of the matter. Then, upon my being appointed Vice Chancellor, I was told that the knighthood was inevitable. The events of the Session and the Queen's departure on her Scotch journey staved it off for the time and I was left tranquil. Some of my friends expressed great uneasiness that I was left the only one of the Vice Chancellors without the honourable appendage to my name. Malins was greatly disquieted. Ellen wished that it should be done. Sis was not pleased, but did not bore me about it. I knew it must come someday, but as I did not wish to accelerate that day I remained wholly silent, and nobody troubled me about it until I received the summons from the Home Secretary.

I went at 9:00 o'clock a.m. to Waterloo station, as I was bidden. I found there Mr. Bruce, Mr. Momsell, Lord de Grey, Lord Sydney (Lord Chamberlain), Mr. Chichester Fortescue, and Mr. Arthur Helps, the Clerk of the Council. There was also a little old man who had grown grey in the service of his country in the War Office, a Mr. Maclean who was going to be knighted as a reward for his having consented to be superseded. A special train carried us to Gosport. A boat there in waiting transferred us to the steamboat. An hour afterwards we were landed on the shore at Osborne, where the Queen's carriages were in waiting, and in which we were carried to the Palace of Osborne. After waiting about half an hour in a drawing room which commanded a beautiful view of the Southern Water and Spithead, we were walked through many passages to the foot of the staircase. There we waited at least another half hour, and the Minister having had interviews with the Queen, the Vice Chancellor was called for. I entered the room in which the Queen was standing with her back to a large window and her face to the door by which I had entered. I approached her bowing and kneeled down before her. She took a sword from Lord Albert Paget, who stood by her side, laid it upon each of my shoulders, and "Sir James." I kissed her hand, rose up, and exited bowing.

We then entered a room in which a lunch or early dinner was served. At the table were my fellow travelers, the Ministers. At the head was the Lord Steward of the Household, at the other end Lord Albert Paget, the Duchess of Athol, two ladies in waiting, a tutor, and the medical attendant of Prince Leopold and several other persons belonging to the household. An excellent plain, plentiful meal – hot leg of mutton and roast fowls, good wine, etc., and being thus refreshed, the Ministers and I and the other new knight again entered the carriages and were transported to the ship and hence to the railway, and so to town before 6:00 o'clock in the evening. And so I was knighted.

Dinner at Lord Cairns, 7 February 1871

Dined out, for the first time, with Lord Cairns, the Duke of Richmond, Lord Stanhope, Lord Mahon, Lord Dufferin, Lord Eustace Cecil, Lord Chelmsford and uxor, Sir Richard Airey and uxor, Mr. Burke and uxor, Sir James Colvin and uxor, Mr. Graham (a young man, a kinsman of Cairns) and uxor, and some others whom I forget.

A pleasant dinner – Lord Stanhope told some of the stories out of Arabia with which he seemed greatly delighted, and some of the audience, to whom they were new, were amused. Lord Chelmsford drew largely upon Joe Miller and the Surrey Sessions. I took an opportunity of mentioning Hawkins's story "But (Opie & Godwin) Neither of Them Took" and I think that fetched them. It was new to all of them and as it was the only new thing they heard that night. I think it was highly successful.

1 November 1871

Travels and Family Affairs

The vacation is over and tomorrow I resume the oar. I have very little to record of the events of the holiday, which has been on the whole less satisfactory than most of those I can remember. A few days after the Court rose in August, Frank and I went to Aix-la-Chapelle. We thought it might do him good – and me no harm – and so it turned out. We went by the afternoon train from Charing Cross to Dover and, the weather being favourable and the appearance of the Ostend boat being attractive, we employed our saunter on the pier, while dinner was preparing, in first making up our minds, and then in securing two berths in a small cabin on the deck. It cost us four or five shillings a piece over the fare and we found it abundantly worth the money. Then, having dined, we embarked at about 10:00 o'clock and after a most easy passage landed at Ostend about half past three o'clock on a very fine morning. We got to a hotel very near the railway station, went to bed, slept soundly till 10:00 o'clock, breakfasted, walked about the town, and saw the bathers and the bathing establishment where the visitors were enjoying the sea breeze and their morning meal and seeming to be well pleased with their fate and their fare.

A famous place for bathing – a very shallow shore and extensive sands – and crowds of people in and out of the water. In dull weather I dare say it must be a dull place, but the bright sunshine and the multitude of pleasure-seekers made it look very agreeable. Dinner at the *table d'hôte* at one – a scrambling meal – and then off by the rail. The rich harvest fields made the flat scenery of Belgium even picturesque occasionally, and always pleasant. It was late – nearly eleven o'clock when we reached Aix. We went to [Hotel] Nuellin, got a very good room, au premier, with two beds in it one of which we dismissed the next morning. I retained mine – Frank found another above stairs, and by this arrangement we were lodged to our hearts' content. Everybody says that Aix is a dull place. I cannot say that I found it disagreeably so. True, you have nothing to do, but then you have your own time to do it in. The country, if not very charming, is not unpleasant nor ugly. There is the Cathedral and the marketplace, and the music at the well and at the redoubt – and the streets and the people and Bernhart's local, where there is not only music but very frequently a play with actors and actresses – none of the best – but as good as at most of the theaters in London, and large veal chops and fried potatoes and food wine from Zellinger to Bramienberger at very moderate prices. If you are very idle and easily pleased, you may live at Aix without finding existence a bore. But if you want rouge et noir and the more exalted and refined delights, which abound at Wiesbaden and Homburg, you must go thither for them. We drank the water punctually. Frank bathed and took lessons in German, I sauntered, smoked at Carolines, and the three weeks to which we had limited our stay passed away without ennui.

We bought some wine from Bernhart, which has since arrived but we have not yet tasted it. We saw but few passengers of our acquaintance. Mr. and Mrs. Harrison lodged in the same hotel. He is a good deal out of health and not the better as he thought for his stay there. The Whitbreads stayed for one day, en route for Wiesbaden. Little Dingy Everitt and his wife and the like – Sergeant Ballantyne and Harry Hawkins flitted through and there was the usual compliment of odd faces and figures at the *table d'hôte*, but nothing worthy of more especial notice. Then we came home. Sis had taken advantage of our absence to have another daughter and was doing quite well. We took the children to Compton, and I had promised myself a very quiet and agreeable vacation there. Shee and his wife paid us a visit, and Hugh and his wife, with Alice arrived from Baxterley. It had been arranged that Sis and her baby should come to us on Saturday, when on getting up on the morning of that day it was ascertained that Annie had an attack of Scarlet Fever. All was dire dismay – I telegraphed to prevent Sis from coming, the children were placed in quarantine. Lawrence came in hot haste from town and carried them all away – and my beautiful plan was utterly demolished.

After a few days, everybody insisted on my going away. I yielded, although I was convinced there was no cause for alarm on my account. Frank had to come to town for revising so he brought me with him and put me out to nurse with the Lawrences, who had taken a house at Folkestone. We left Hugh and Annie in possession of Compton. The fever, which appears to have been but slight, had its way and Annie was very soon out of all danger. But she was for some weeks in that state of peeling which is said to be most formidable for the chance of infection. However, she got quite well and went after about four weeks to her mother at Brighton and is now reinstated at Baxterley.

And so we passed five weeks at Folkstone – a time of pure idleness – very fine weather. Some very pleasant drives in the neighborhood, but without any event worth recollecting, except only that in an excursion to Lyminge I found in the parson there, and old friend, Mr. Jenkyns, who, more than 30 years ago, was the youthful curate at Willesden. We were glad to meet, and the meeting brought back to me some sweet and bitter recollections. Poor dear Laura had a great liking for him, and we were for some time in great intimacy. Then he married a Miss Finch, the daughter of one of the rich moneyers of the Mint who had formed a sort of colony at Neasden and the neighbourhood. He got a living somewhere and departed, and I saw him no more until I found him in his curious old church, founded by a Royal Saxon Saint – Ethelburga – whose burial place and memory he seemed to have a great veneration for. I believe he is a learned divine and addicted to polemical controversy. He gave me (besides a little antiquarian tract on the history of his church) a profound criticism of the Pope's dogma on the Immaculate Conception, in which he would seem to have the better of His Holiness if the whole current of Ecclesiastical authority which he quotes could be of any avail against infallibility.

We came to town about the middle of October - and then paid a visit of ten days to Arden at Rickmansworth. Very quiet and agreeable but sadly broken off by the illness of poor Rose Thornton, who was obliged to depart suddenly. On her reaching home, she was for some days in considerable danger but has happily escaped, although not wholly restored. I hope, however, that she is now doing well, and that time and quiet will set her to rights.

My poor sister Betsy, upon whom years and infirmities had been accumulating became dangerously ill. Her sisters were constant in their attendance upon her. She was provided with a nurse and with all that could relieve and comfort her, but the hour had come and in November she ended peacefully and resigned and left the existence of which she had fulfilled all the duties of daughter, sister and wife in a most exemplary manner. Handsome in person, strong, active and laboriously industrious, and gifted with excellent good sense and possessing natural talents which greater advantages of education and society would have made brilliant, she was for years the mainstay of our large and burdensome family. Honestly proud, but not in the least vain, the narrowness of our early circumstances never led her to repine, or to relax in those unselfish exertions to which we all owed so much if an arduous but well spent life can entitle human beings to any reward hereafter as our steadfast belief is. I doubt not that she is enjoying it, and that her pious resignation to God's will must ensure her His abundant grace and mercy. Amen!

Back to Business

The Chancellor's (Hatherley) troubles consequent upon his and Gladstone's tricky appointment of [Robert] Collier to the Bench of the Common Pleas (in order that he might be removed to the Privy Council, as he was after a few days) forced upon the Lord Chancellor the necessity of appointing a Common Law Judge in the place of poor Hayes, whose post had remained vacant ever since his death, three years ago. Cockburn's letters to the Lord Chancellor and to Gladstone had made an inconvenient stir. Still the Lord Chancellor was obstinate, still he stuck to his foolish, fatal notion that there were too many Common Law Judges, and that to save a salary would justify him in the eye of God and man. And harking back upon the sublime idea which had regulated his scheme when he had resolved to turn me adrift and to appoint Branwell, or some other Common Law Judge, to the office of Chief Justice in Bankruptcy, he bethought himself that since he must appoint a judge, he could make him undertake the Bankruptcy as part of his office. As this could not be done while I held the latter appointment, he wrote to me suggesting that I should give it up and confine myself to the duties of Vice Chancellor. This I could have no objection – rather the contrary, for although I can only do a day's work in a day, and it matters nothing to me whether I do that in Lincoln's Inn or in Lincoln's Inn Fields – I should not be unwilling to sit as Vice Chancellor without interruption. But this rather for the Bar than for my personal convenience. So I replied to his letter, expressing my readiness to accede to any arrangement which he thought would be advantageous to the public service, but begged him to let it be understood that my ceasing to be Chief Justice in Bankruptcy was neither because I was tired of my office nor because he was tired of me.

I believe he proposed this in a letter to Cockburn, and I suppose it satisfied him that a Common Law Judge has quite enough to do without enlarging the sphere of his activity. However, this may have been the Lord Chancellor who wrote to me to say that the judges made such difficulties about these circuits that he must forego his intention. And so things remain as they were and he has been compelled against his will to appoint a Judge in the Queen's Bench, and for this has selected little Quain. who thus obtains a reward for his radical excursions at London University, his retirement as a candidate when he was put up to oppose Lowe and his mischievous doctrinaire labours in Judicature Common. May he "purge and live cleanly!"

Hugh and his wife – with Alice and little Jem – paid me a visit in December. Annie is perfectly restored to health and Hugh cooling down from the excitement he has been in, occasioned by a vacancy in the grown living at Nuneaton, to which some of his friends in the country had made up their minds he was likely to be appointed. In my opinion, nothing was more improbable, and I may add (not because the grapes are sour) that I should have thought it by no means desirable for him. A larger income but then a much larger parish with several curates, abundant dissent, and opportunities for quarrelling, which he is much better for being out of the way of. All for the best! However, I am afraid that it disturbed his equanimity – though I must say that he put a good face on it and seems to be pretty well reconciled to his lot. I believe his wife rejoices at what he would fain persuade himself is a disappointment and has the good sense to see that a quiet and independent life, with a competence, is preferable to a more conspicuous but at the same time a more laborious and exacting occupation.

Christmas 1871

And all this brought us to Christmas, and a rare Christmas Day we had! The children and their father and mother and Rose Thornton and Mr. Arden came to dine with us. Frank had ransacked his invention and rifled the stores of the Co-operative Association for toys and bon-bons and surprises for young and old. And if success is a sufficient reward for a world of trouble, verily he had his reward. The bright eyes of the children, and their shouts of delight were beyond all price. More splendid entertainments no doubt there were many on this festive occasion, but a more thoroughly joyous one, to those whom it most concerned I don't think the wide world could produce.

And so ended Christmas and the year 1871 for all that has been good in which may Heaven make us thankful – to all that we think other than good may Heaven make us resigned – and for all may Heaven make us thankful for the past- and hopeful for the future.

Home at Compton and More Travels

June 1872

Very seldom does it happen – such is the course of my life – that I have a time to myself, a period in which I have no companions but my own thoughts, and without making invidious comparisons between such moments, and the more usual busy periods of my existence, I am bound to confess that I enjoy more durable and tranquil enjoyment from the rarer intervals than from the more common employment of my time. On Thursday (the 13th June), I left town to spend a few days at Compton. The weather, which had been simply detestable, cloudy and rainy and cold, for several weeks before had changed its mind. The morning was comparatively clear and quite calm, improved during the journey, and upon arriving at my destination I found it perfectly pleasant – warm and bright. The garden was a delight – the bright sun, the flowers, the leafy trees, and the pure balmy air made me forget the noise and gloom in which I had been living. I wandered through the garden and the fields with as much pleasure as if I had never seen them before and dined face to face with the sidelong glories of the setting sun and passed an evening full of tranquil enjoyment.

As the light diminished, then faded, and at length declined, the varying aspects of the garden were full of interest. At first a blaze of bright light fell upon the trees on the left bank and made them glow in such brightness as only the sun's rays can bestow. By slow degrees the brightness was less strong and the golden colours faded a little, the bright greens declined into a russet tent – still distinct and clear in outline and in shade – and as the sun sank in the West and fell below the horizon, the golden and red and brown colours sank into a cool grey. The stems of the first and the yews being the last to yield up the brightness which had been cast upon or brought out of them. At length one grey tint covered the whole scene, intense only where the masses of foliage retained its strength and softening off until it differed little from the color of the sky at the extremities. Then a perfect quiet assumed its rain. The birds, which had been shouting in noisy rivalry became mute, some few thrushes and blackbirds only occasionally uttering a defiant "good night" and soon afterwards all was wholly silent. All nature seems to sink into glad repose. A sacred calm comes over my spirits, disturbed only by the ever-present pain which accompanies the thoughts of my past happiness – a past never to return.

When we were at Compton at Whitsuntide, Frank and I conceived the notion that we might make our next visit by way of the Thames with this view we went to Oxford – and there after some inquiry we found a man who undertook to bring a houseboat, with a horse, to Maidenhead at such time as we might fix on and transport us thence to Oxford, stopping as often as we might choose on the way. After a time, this design was imparted to the children – their imagination at once took fire – and for weeks before the beginning of the vacation nothing was talked or thought about but the delight of such a voyage as we contemplated. At length the time came – the 5th of August – Sis would fain have gone with us, but poor Tertius had suffered miserably from an attack of gout and was recommended to go to Carlsbad (as he did on the 8th) and so our troop consisted only of Frank and I, the four children, and their maid Henriette.

We set off by rail to Maidenhead, arrived in the midst of a violent rain, and scrambled along and flew to the place where our ship (the *Water Lily*) was moored and we were greatly disappointed at finding that instead of the houseboat which we had seen at Oxford, the skipper had brought us a large punt, which in the then state of the weather filled us with alarm. It did not, however, turn out so badly as we feared – we had a good roof, the sides were pretty well protected with curtains, tarpaulin, and an extra blanket. We resolved to go on, and so we did. As I have recorded the particulars of our voyage in an epistle to Sis, I shall not repeat them here – only lest I should forget matters so deeply interesting that I remind myself that we slept the first night at Henley, the second at Pangbourne, the third at Abingdon, and reached Oxford at one o'clock p.m. on the fourth day. I think I may say we all enjoyed the trip in spite of the weather, which, to say the least of it, was not kind. If it had been fine, perhaps it would have been too delightful.

We drove from Oxford to Compton and arrived in time for tea. There we settled down. The weather took up and was bright and beautiful for several weeks – all the time of the harvest. Shee and his wife came to us for a fortnight. I paid a visit to my brother Malins at Purely Hall. The Dickinsons came to see us, he being, as I hope and believe, thoroughly recovered from his most dangerous illness. After that the Whitbreads came (No, they came before the Dickinsons), and then Sis and Tertius arrived, quite well and satisfied with the effect of the Carlsbad waters. And so we went on, doing nothing, and enjoying the operation until the 12th of

October, when Sis and her children went to London and I to Bath. (A miserable account of the garden – no apples, no plums, or indeed any other fruit than a few uneatable pears. McQueen has departed and appears to have left the kitchen garden in a most unsatisfactory condition – no winter stock). There I stayed, drinking the water and bathing till the 26th. Frank, who had been in London revising, joined me on the 15th. We were comfortably lodged at the Grand Pump Room Hotel, and although the weather was not of the best we managed to make it out pretty well. Somewhat dull but between walking and going to see the country, which is full of charming views, especially from the hill above Box – Warleigh and from Bradford-on-Avon, we managed to get through the time. The panorama from the height above Bradford is very fine – a long range of downs in the distance, not unlike ours and with a White Horse too a fine valley Trowbridge, Westbury, Warminster, etc.

I wrote to Chief Justice [Sir Alexander] Cockburn congratulating him on his "Reasons," respecting the Geneva Arbitration [of the *Alabama* Claims]. He sent me a full copy of the document (I had before only seen extracts in the newspapers) and I found his card on returning to town. He is the only person, as far as I at present know, who has spoken out and told the truth about this miserable affair, and I think he deserves high honour for having maintained the dignity of the nation and the credit of our profession – and this in the tone and with the spirit of an English gentleman.

Then I found that R[oundell] Palmer was appointed Lord Chancellor. I wrote to congratulate him, which I did with perfect sincerity – and not for his own merits alone – although I think they fairly entitle him to the promotion, but also because I feel that this court of Chancery is relieved by the retirement of Lord Hatherley, whom I consider the most dangerous enemy to the Court of Chancery, and who, if he had stayed, would have attempted more mischief still. Holidays are over. Saturday's Term begins.

Fresh woods and pastures now.

26 November 1872, Tuesday

More Work, Old Colleagues

The term is over, without having produced anything at all remarkable. Dull, dull – not quite stagnant – but without a ripple on the surface. As Monday was the last seal, I devoted this day to Bankruptcy and cleared off a tolerably long paper. Had a common law case (E. P. Childers, I think) with Russell, Q.C. on one side and Cohen on the other. Sufficiently out of the common run of Bankruptcy cases to be of some interest. (What a wonderful thing the common law is! What a wonderful collection of instances does *Smith's Leading Cases* present of common sense and common honesty being made to give place to the curiosities of special pleading!) I did my best to make the former prevail, but probably the Lords Justice may prefer the latter.

News of the death of poor John Osborne – he had better have stayed, and worked, than to take a Criminal Court Judgeship. His happiness was not improved, and I doubt not his death was accelerated by his retirement. *Il l'a voulu*. Who can tell? A good tempered honest, manly fellow.

The Common Law Judges are greatly exercised, and the Common Pleas greatly divided in respect of a Criminal Case before them. A knock 'em down man at a fair walked off with the sovereign, which a loser of 6d. had given him to get changed. Qu: did he steal 19/6?, and the judges doubt whether he has been properly convicted!!

5 December 1872

Dinner at Keating's. Many judges and more lawyers of all kinds and degrees. Lord Chelmsford told all the old stories which I have heard repeated so often that I have forgotten them all until I hear them over again. The only story I heard that had a smack of novelty (to me) was from Blackburn about Lord Braxfield, whose name – his dignity laid aside – was just McQueen. A favorite and faithful butler who had lived with him many years came to him one morning and said he was sorry to say he must leave his service. "How's that, John?" said his lordship, "what have you to complain of?" "Oh naething, my Lord, as far as concerns your lordship

– you have always been very kind and considerate – but Mrs. McQueen's temper is so dreadful that I can't live with her." "Old man," said his Lordship, "what would you do if you were married to her?"   Lord, after the above was written, in this January 1887, the public papers announce that Blackburn has resigned, or is about to resign his post as one of the Lords of Appeal in the House of Lords – a post which he has occupied for a good many years. He has the deserved reputation of being a good lawyer, that is to say he is well acquainted with all the cases which have been decided by judges who preceded him in office, and he has been at all times resolute in applying the principles which are to be deduced from former decisions. If there are to be found in his decisions, which have been numerous and in many very important cases, any trace of an enlarged, philosophical, or even general view of what the grounds of such decisions ought to be, I have been unable to discover it. No one can say that he is an attractive man. He is usually taciturn, not ready to venture any opinion of his own, and not appearing to value if he condescends to reply to the opinions of other persons, he is very well contented with himself and not convinced that what anybody else may say or think is worthy of consideration.

On ceasing to be in the House of Lords, his peerage merely burns out. He is no longer in, or of, the House. He will remain Lord Blackburn. I don't think he will be missed. I don't see any reason why he should be mourned, or why the extinction of his forensic authority should be more important than that of the cigar from which he seems to derive all the enjoyment he is capable of experiencing.

January 1887

Privy Council

At the end of the sittings – when the Vacation of 1886 began – I was thoroughly tired. I am not so ill as to prevent my performing my public duty as easily as I had been accustomed to do, but I was tired, thoroughly tired of doing the same kind of thing, day after day the whole course of my life, presenting no change or producing any excitement. I was too sensible that the change was in myself, and that the fault, if fault there was, was in me – in my waxing years and my failing strength and fading spirits.

I was encouraged and cheered by the dear ones who surrounded me and who did for me all that affection and duty prompted. Everybody congratulated me on "looking so well." Everything external was pleasant and happy. I was thankful and happy so far as the means of happiness were within my reach. Quiet and retirement improved my health. But I could not walk, I could not join in the cheerful pleasures which all about me were enjoying. The pleasures of memory were saddened by the recollection of joys which had been and which can never return. I no longer slept as I had been used to do. My appetite had lost its force in flavour. My physical infirmities were sensibly increased and increasing and I became convinced that I had become in plain English a helpless old man. I therefore determined after long and serious meditation to give up my office but not without very great reluctance, nor until after long deliberation with my dear children who are and always have been my dearest friends and most disinterested and faithful counselors. I postponed taking this most important step for the moment and resolved upon trying what might be the result of my attempt to resume my duties for some short time.

In this state of things, I returned to town at the close of October 1886. Having sat in Court for some weeks, I became convinced that I ought not to continue, so to avoid all the risks which might otherwise ensue I determined to communicate my wishes to the Lord Chancellor and wrote to him on 5 December 1886. A day or two afterwards, he came to my room and in very friendly terms expressed his regret at the intention I had communicated to him. He requested me not to announce that intention for some short time and stated very frankly that he was somewhat embarrassed in selecting my successor. Several persons were named but for none of them did he express any predilection excepting McNaughten – [who he] said had already refused several offers of preferment which had been made to him but who said was the fittest by far of all whose names had been mentioned.

It is not worthwhile to recollect what was said in this confidential talk as to the several other persons who were mentioned, but certainly he was greatly in doubt as to all of them except McNaughten, with whom he said in conclusion that he thought he should enter into diplomatic communication. I would not have it understood that he consulted me as to the choice he had to make but our talk was quite free and unrestrained as between old friends upon a subject which both of us thought of serious interest and public importance. I took the opportunity at the end of our conference of saying that I should be greatly pleased at being admitted a member of the Privy Council. This he said he thought I was entitled to ask for and promised to speak about it to [the Prime Minister] Lord Salisbury.

In compliance with the Lord Chancellor's request, I did not mention my intended retirement to anyone – that continued my attendance at Court as usual until about ten days afterwards, when I received a note from him accepting my resignation and informing me that I was to be named to the Privy Council. At about the same time, I received a note from Lord Salisbury informing me that Her Majesty had been pleased so to appoint me.

Being thus freed from all the restraints I had imposed upon myself, I resolved to announce my retirement to the Bar and in open court. I had intended to do this with as little formality or fuse as possible and sent on the morning of the one of my ordinary cards to the courts of the several judges with "P.C." [i.e. Privy Councilor] in the corner, meaning merely to say "Good-bye" to each of them as my old friends. To my great astonishment, all such of them as had come to their courts visited me in my room and with most kind and hearty expressions of goodwill (which I can never forget) insisted upon accompanying me in court and being present at my leave-taking.

On taking my seat, the Attorney General (Richard Webster) rose and made me a very kind and too flattering speech in the name of the Bar, who by this time had collected in such numbers as filled the court. I replied as well as I could and then withdrew. Thus ended my reign as Vice Chancellor!

I need not write anymore about the proceedings of this day because several of the newspapers contain rather full accounts of all that was said and done, and I believe Frank has made a collection of extracts which tell the whole story. I received many most kind letters of congratulation – not only enough, but more than enough to satisfy my utmost vanity – and to make me believe that I am fortunate enough to be held in esteem by persons whose regard and goodwill are most gratifying to me. These letters I believe Frank has preserved.

On being summoned, I went to Windsor. On the platform at the railway, I found Lord Cranbrook, Lord Cross, the Clerk of the Council, Lord Peel, Lord Rosyn and Sir Georg Bowen (a colonial officer of long standing), who was going on the lake errand with myself to Windsor. We were installed in a state carriage and the trip was passed very pleasantly. The two first named lords I knew very well. Lord Roslyn knew me because his wife was the mother of two young ladies, wards of court, and I had had many dealings in Chambers with their fortunes (which were very large) during their respective infancies. It was all about squeezing as much as possible out of the income under the colour of keeping up the mansion, repairing furniture, keeping up domestic supplies and many other ingenious contrivances which I am not quite sure were always so much for the benefits of the infants as for increasing the revenue of their mother and next friend. Perhaps I may have cut down some of these well-meant contrivances. If I did, he must have known all about it. However, he did not appear to bear me any malice. On the contrary, he was a very cheerful well-bred gentleman – remarkably good-looking – with an arabesque grey mustache which would account for any good-looking young widow as his lady was, taking a fancy to him.

The journey passed pleasantly enough. At the Windsor station, we got into Royal Carriages and were transferred to the Castle.

After waiting about half an hour in a gorgeous saloon, we were taken through the somewhat intricate galleries and passages – very gorgeous in colour and gilding and adorned with many pictures and busts – to a sort of resting place from which after some further waiting we were admitted to a small chamber in which H. M. the Queen was sitting on a small sofa with a low table before her. Here the Clerk of the Council, standing, read the oaths of the allegiance and of the Privy Council to us three kneeling: Lord Roslyn, myself, and Sir George Bowen. Each of us, as we were respectively sworn, kissed the hand of Her Majesty and then shook hands with each of the elder Privy Council their present, and, bowing to the Queen, backed out of the presence. And so ended that ceremony. We then went back through the passages (corridors I ought to call them), reached a dining room, had a plentiful and cheerful repast, and back to London in the same carriage and with the same companions.

Last Thoughts and Recollections

Appendix A: Further memories of the Court of Bankruptcy
4 October 1868

Well, it was bad enough to see [Sir Richard] Malins a Vice Chancellor and [Charles] Selwyn a [Lord Justice of Appeal]. Nothing could be more convincing than that preferment in the Court of Chancery was regulated not by a comparison of men's merits (I say this to myself, and with a perfect conviction that vanity does not prompt me – whatever other people may think), but by the influence of party politics, and perhaps of mere accident. I don't persuade myself and I would not condescend to try to persuade others that I am so far superior to the two I have named as that their appointment was unjust. They are just as good as I am, but they are of much less standing and there can be no reason to any impartial person why they should have been preferred to me and to others, except only political influence and accident. The chances turned out well for them – they were against me – I have no right therefore to complain, nor did I ever, nor do I complain.

        Then came another chance. [William] Wood's promotion to Lord Chancellor [as Lord Hatherley] made a vacancy for Vice Chancellor. [George] Giffard was appointed. There could not have been a better appointment. He is a gentleman, which I think an indispensable requisite, and he is master of his business, just and manly and generous and bold. But he is of less standing than I and as far as I know (but of this I am not a competent judge) not of any higher reputation than I was. Still, I have no right nor reason to complain of this appointment. Some of my friends – perhaps only to console me – said I was passed over because I was thought to be too old. If this was the true reason I have no right to complain of that, but it could not be the true reason, for, old though I am, I am not older than many men who have been when raised to a similar post – and I am not aware of any such external mark of senility, or of any deficiency in the discharge of duties in Court as should justly excite a doubt of my being able to fulfill the office of judge. The extent of my business was equal to that of any practitioner, and I don't believe that I had exhibited any failure of intelligence or activity or ability.

This suggestion, however, set me upon thinking seriously that (all ambition being dead in me and all hope being, after what had happened, wholly extinguished) the time had come when it would be well to retire while yet I could do so without incurring the suspicion of being driven away. I had (I may truly say) the best place in Vice Chancellor Stuart's Court. To maintain that position, very considerable exertions were absolutely necessary. Sitting up late at night was rather more than my strength sufficed, for the attendance upon two and sometimes three Courts was distressing to my spirits. Several younger and able men were hanging upon my skirts and treading on my heels. A week's illness might do me irretrievable mischief, and leave my retreat less graceful and much less agreeable to my feelings than if it were made "not upon compulsion."

For these reasons I had, after much thought, and much talk upon the subject with those whose affection no less than their judgment I could rely, determined that I would not make my appearance at the Bar after the long vacation. On the day the Court rose, I went into Cairn's room simply to wish him good-bye and a pleasant holiday. "Stay awhile," said he. "No," I said, "you have plenty to do and I have not quite finished my work – and I have said all I have to say to you." "Sit down for a minute," said he, pulling off his wig and gown. I took a chair, and he having dressed sent his secretaries and the other people standing about out of the room. He then said to me that [Edward] Goulburn was about to resign his office of Commissioner of Bankruptcy and that his health was such as that he could not hold his office under any circumstances for many weeks. He asked if I would accept the post, saying several very kind things about it being less than my merits entitled me too, which it is unnecessary here to set down. Being in the frame of mind I have before described, I accepted his offer readily and thankfully. About a month after this, he wrote to me saying he had just heard of Goulburn's death and offered me the appointment. I answered immediately accepting it and was sworn in. Holroyd was then the Vacation Commissioner, which he continued to be until the 30 September, and on the 1st of October I assumed the functions of Commissioner of Bankruptcy.

I write this because memory is so little to be trusted that unless things are recorded about the time they happened, there is great hazard of their being imperfectly recollected, and whether or not they are pretty sure to be misunderstood and misrepresented.

Note to Appendix A, April 1890

I wrote these scraps at the time they bear date. Sometimes afterwards, I appear to have written at greater length and probably have repeated in part at least. If I have time, I will try to bring this story into better order. In the meantime, what I have scribbled must be taken as my then impression.

Last Travels

We made several journeyings during the long vacations. I don't know very well how we came to spend so much money and so much time in these trips. We were very comfortable at home, but we were tempted by that love of change which is common, I suppose, to all persons who are troubled with active imaginations and in the enjoyment of good health and spirits.

> Le désir de voir, et l'humeur inquiète, l'emporterent enfin…

And we set out with light hearts and firm determinations to be pleased. The remembrances of our adventures, dim as most of them have become, have left so many agreeable impressions that I could not forgive myself if I omitted to mention some of them in this collection of memories.

I am indebted greatly to dearest Sis for the dates and names of the places we visited on several of these occasions – without her most essential help I should not have been able to trace our wanderings with any approach to accuracy. In August 1852, our party consisted of my wife, Sis, and myself. We crossed at Calais and proceeded directly to Brussels and thence to Chaudfontaine in the beautiful valley of the Vesdre crossing the Meuse at Liège. I do not think we stayed in that city but the sight of it reminded us of Quentin Durward and the wild doings of the Boer of Ardenne, which Sir Walter Scott was immortalized in his history which if it is not historically true it ought to be.

At Chaudfontaine, I was unwell and we were compelled to stay there for a couple of days. I supposed I had eaten something that did not agree with me (perhaps some apricots about which I feel rather guilty). We proceeded to Aix-la-Chapelle, where the warm baths and the estimable Dr. Hermann soon set me to rights. After a few days, we went on to Cologne, visited the grand Cathedral, which was not then completed as it has since been to the great credit of the country to which it is a lasting honour. We duly paid our respects to the eleven thousand virgins![13] Of course we sacrificed at the Shrine of the Nymphs *"gegenüber dem Jülichs-Platz"*[14] and embarked upon the steamboat, enjoying greatly the beautiful, varied, and picturesque scenery on both banks of the magnificent Rhine.

Thus we reached Frankfurt, examined the streets and squares, Goethe's father's house, and the *Judengasse*, the nest of the Rothschilds from which sprung that wonderful bird, the Phoenix of modern finance, whose brood seems likely under the magic power of gold to buy up the whole world or at least to make all its inhabitants holders of shares and coupons. From Frankfurt to Munich, we availed ourselves of the railway stopping at Würzburg – home to the stein wine of which is, to my liking, the best of all that I have tasted in this most wine-drinking country. We did not forget to visit the tomb of the great *Minnesänger* [Walther von der Vogelweide], whose dulcet melody is said to have been of power "to while the bird from off the bough." We slept, I think, at Augsburg and saw the house of the Fuggers, the great moneychangers, and the fireplace in which tradition says that the magnificent banker, after entertaining the Emperor Charles V at a sumptuous banquet, tossed into the blazing cinnamon fuel (no less) a large bundle of the bonds by which the Emperor acknowledged himself to be a debtor for millions. A receipt in full of all demands!!! In our days, I suppose the financier would have swapped the bonds for a concession of a score of railway lines, or thousand miles of auriferous rocks in South Africa.

Munich we found full of interest and beauty. The gallery is full of good pictures. It would be impossible to do it justice without a long enumeration of the admirable works it contains, but I can never forget the delight with which I contemplated some of the earlier, less known, and

---

[13] Bacon refers to the Christian tale of the 11,000 virgins led by St. Ursula, who were said to have been martyred at Cologne in the fourth century.
[14] A famous Cologne perfume shop

smaller works of Rubens. I have not now the time nor the means of attempting to tell all the wonders I saw, or the great pleasure which we, the travelers, derived from the contemplation of the never-to-be-forgotten marvels which lined the walls of these galleries. We could not wholly repress some feelings of envy at finding the sculptures from Egypt deposited here, instead of being placed as they ought to have been in company with our Elgin marbles, nor some touch of anger and disappointment at the careless mismanagement of our agents who let slip the opportunity of securing for us the possession of such treasures.

With all my love of art, it would not be right to close all I have to say about Munich if I did not devote a line to the merit of Bavarian beer. It is one of the pleasantest and most innocent drinks I am acquainted with. To the taste delicious, to the stomach invigorating, to the brain stimulating without being exciting. It deserves all that Milton (who was a good judge of excellence in eating and drinking) makes Comus[15] say of his cup. Not that Nepentha, the wife of Thome in Egypt, gave to Jove-born Helena was of such power to stir up joy as this to life so friendly, and so cool to thirst.

When we had exhausted the beauties of Munich – the streets, the public buildings, the Pinakothek [art gallery], the museums, the mural paintings of Cornelius and others, we set about continuing our travels. Salzburg was to be our next stopping place. We hired a carriage which was to take us thither in three days. We found the hotel full – some revel was going – and Sis found herself for the first time in a brilliantly lighted *salle à manger* filled with a smoking, drinking crowd. However, all went well.

We were hungry and tired, and having satisfied our craving appetites, we retired early to very tolerable bedrooms. The next day took us to Reichenthal, and on the third day we reached Salzburg. All I can recollect of this trajet is that we passed through a varied and interesting country, that the weather was very fine, and that we were in that condition of good health and spirits which enabled us to enjoy the novelties and the ease of our position. We visited the churches and public buildings and the other lions of this famous old city, which it would be tedious here to mention. Our next course was to pass through the Salzkammergut and the first remarkable thing we saw was the Salt mine at Hallein, we had been

---

[15] In Greek mythology, the son of Bacchus and Circe

enjoined not to miss. Well, we did this to order. We had to don the coarse, dirty-looking costume of the working miners, a very necessary process for, among other reasons, the preservation of our clothes which would have been spoiled if we had exposed them to the damp and dirt of the subterranean passages we had to thread. Down, down slippery ladder-like slopes, in the clutch of the sturdy miners without whose help I dare not think what might have become us. We came to a dismal, phantasmagoric lake the opposite shore of which was lighted by innumerable bills or lamps which displayed the crystal stalactites of the roof and sides of the doleful cavern to which we were introduced. However, as all things must have an end, we accomplished our dismal pilgrimage and, after much clambering and sliding and slipping, we were restored to the light of day.

This was my first visit to a mine, as it was the first of my companions, and I mentally resolved never willingly to repeat the experiment. Let no one be tempted by the description of tourists, or the desire of seeing something altogether new, to go down a mine, for there is much labour and even danger in such an exploit – pleasure there is none – and anyone who has a good-sized coal-cellar of his own made by shutting himself in it, and blowing out his candle reproduce all the sensations, if not all the excitement which can be afforded by an adventure in the far-famed salt mine of Hallein. The only amusement we found was in contemplating the squalid and grotesque figures we presented in the daylight before we cast off the filthy and ugly costumes in which we had been encased. Oh, for a photographer! Such a metamorphosis. As they say in Ireland, "Our own dog would not have known us."

The rest of the journey through the Salt District was indescribably beautiful. Endless variety of fertile plains, mountains, rocks, and lakes diversified the scenes we passed through in journeying by Berchtesgaden, Gmunden, and Isehl to Linz. Among the points too numerous to attempt a description I cannot forget the lake on the way to Isehl, where the lofty black rocks rose precipitously from the dark deep water and seemed to wall in the steamboat.

At Linz, we embarked on the steamboat for Vienna. The voyage on the great river was most delightful. The deep rolling stream, the castles and villas on either side, placed with great judgment and taste at points and upon headlands commanding admirable views of the reaches and turnings of the water course, the shining cheerful towns and villages – the busy navigation with boats of various sizes and descriptions presented objects of infinite variety and interest – and made the passage appear much shorter than it really was. From Neuberg, where we landed, to Vienna the distance was some miles – I forget how many, but it was soon passed and we found ourselves comfortably lodged in a good hotel in a lively quarter of Vienna after a most satisfactory voyage.

Of course in the morning we set about seeing the sights and wonders (and there are many) of this famous city. We visited the most remarkable Cathedral of St. Stephen, one of the most impressive of the cathedrals I have ever seen, and verified the truth and vigour of Stanfield's painting. We went to see the Royal Cemetery, a most elaborate and imposing resting place for the departed Majesty of Austria, where I remember my dear wife caught a cold that for some days greatly interfered with our pleasures. We saw the great armoury, full of warlike weapons and appliances ancient and modern. We went to Schönbrunn, once the residence of Napoleon's son who there terminated his short, ill-starred existence.[16] We dwelled as long as we could, but not as long as they deserved, upon the matchless pictures in the Esterházy and Liechtenstein Galleries. But why should I try to recollect or to attempt my detailed account of the fine and noble things which delighted us at Vienna? They may be read in Murray's *Handbook*,[17] and I do not wish to make a guidebook of my recollections.

From Vienna, we went by the then somewhat new railway to the ancient city of Prague. The situation is most remarkable, and the old part of the city full of historical associations. The walls of the palace inhibited by the ferocious, ambitious, and superstitious Wallenstein revived our recollections of the dreadful times in which he [Friedrich] Schiller has conferred an immortality upon that man in those times. The austere synagogue, with its shrines and candle sticks (said to be genuine and

---

[16] Napoleon's son with his second wife, Archduchess Marie Louise of Austria, was confined there for most of his life, dying of tuberculosis at age 21, in 1832.
[17] Murray's *Handbooks for Travellers* series was a standard travel guide for British tourists published from 1836 to 1911.

brought from Jerusalem), and the burial place of the Jews were duly visited, and at least, wondered at. A more dismal looking place than the latter can hardly be conceived – a station of despair, not only apparently neglected but degraded.

From Prague, we passed through the so-called Saxon Switzerland.[18] Why so-called I cannot explain – any resemblance to the land of William Tell I failed to perceive. There are, no doubt, many points of wild picturesqueness – accidents in which masses of rock and scattered groups of trees might furnish materials to landscape painters do abound, but as it appeared to me a total absence of the grave mysterious consistency which constitutes the dignity and majesty of Swiss scenery – which makes it the despair of the painter – while scores of good and telling pictures might be made of the morsels not unsparingly furnished by parts of the Saxon Switzerland.

We here reached the Elbe, which soon brought us to Dresden. To describe the gallery would be wholly out of place here. The guidebooks contain many items of great interest, and the catalogues are full of notices of all the pictures. Travelers, as we were, could only gaze with delight upon the grand and beautiful and interesting treasures which the walls display. The great Raphaels – the Sistine Madonna, familiar as its forms and features were to us by means of the numerous copies and engravings, surpassed all that we had imagined. Correggios of remarkable excellence – many Wouwermans in his very best style, other Low Country masters, Canalettos, and a multitude of others pleased us greatly, and even bewildered us somewhat by their numbers. Although I give up the task of noticing them more particularly, I can never forget the pleasure I derived from looking at and now recalling their excellence. From Dresden, we went to Leipzig, the great bookselling mart of literary Germany, and the scene of Auerbach's cellar (in *Faust*) but which we had not time to visit or to look for, although I am told it is kept up to this day with a sort of veneration. At Weimar (Goethe's residence) we made a short stay and then passed Erfurt and Cassel to Frankfurt and thence to Paris.

---

[18] A rural area in Saxony still known as such today due to its resemblance to Switzerland, even if Bacon did not appreciate it.

We arrived at Paris when that most lively city was in gala. We secured lodgings in a hotel on the Boulevard des Italiens, at which we agreed was a somewhat extravagant charge, but which we did not regret since the object of our travel was to see all we could. And there, at our ease in a commodious balcony and above the heads of the surging crowds that filled the streets we saw a very grand military procession. Its principal feature was the unlucky Napoleon III, in honour of whom the *fête* was held and in celebration of his recent inspection of troops in garrison. There he rode and triumphed in glory, caracoling on a magnificent white charger – bowing to his faithful (?) subjects, who rent the air with their shouts and "heedless of the coming whirlwind's sway, which hushed in grim repose, expects its evening pray." What a contrast between the brilliant glory of that day's triumph and the disastrous defeat and submission of Sedan,[19] where the rash gamester lost his last stake!

Further Memories of Travel in France

In 1853 we tried a fresh country. On this occasion, my poor boy James was added to our last year's party. We went first to Paris and thence by easy journeys to Bordeaux. We stayed for a while at Orléans and saw the churches and the museum and all that we could cram into our rambling about the town. We were all good walkers in those days, and all in good health and spirits, and quite ready to be pleased and amused at all we saw or met with. We talked much about Jeanne d'Arc and the exploits of Talbot Salisbury and the wars that Shakespeare chronicled for all. We were greatly delighted with the glimpses we occasionally got of the Loire, stopped at Angoulême and at Poitiers, both of which in spite of modern improvements retain something of a Middle Age shape and colour. Different no doubt from the appearance they gave in the days of Froissart,[20] but with the help of a busy imagination we contrived to persuade ourselves that we were travelling over his very ground.

Bordeaux pleased us greatly. The present Bordeaux is unquestionably a very fine city. The wide streets, the elegant structures

---

[19] Napoleon III's great defeat in September 1870, where his army was defeated and he captured after failing in an attempt to be killed on the field.
[20] A great chronicler of medieval France

public and private, the churches, theatre, and not the least the magnificent bridge over the Garonne commanded our admiration. And the river itself – the shipping and the busy quays were full of activity and interest. A part of Bordeaux forms a singular and picturesque contrast to the stately edifices of the new city, which owes its glory to the taste and skill of Mansard and the other able architects of *le siècle de Louis XIV*, and his immediate successor [Louis XV]. When we had feasted our eyes and refreshed our memories with the beauties and amusements of this most remarkable city, we proceeded through the pine forest and the now lying Landes to Bayonne. That has undergone much less change. It has an air of antiquity which pleased me much. It is less exclusively French and more Spanish than any other town we had seen. We of course made acquaintance with the celebrated chocolate of which we had heard so much, as everybody has, for which this place is so much noted, but with every respect for the genius of the place I am not sure that we did not drink as good in Paris.

From Bayonne we drove to San Sebastian where we passed a night. All was now changed. We were decidedly in Spain. The coast, the town of Passages, and the stout and able boatwomen who were there performing the maritime labours, which are elsewhere usually assigned to the other sex, claimed our admiration. It is impossible to look or to think unmoved at the formidable fortress, and the scene of one of the most celebrated exploits of British arms, where the artillery upon the heights poured its fire over the heads of our advancing columns as they swarmed to the attack when the fortress was taken by assault. Here fell that young Follet, whom his brothers – our dear friends – never mentioned without tears and who, though they were justly proud of Sir William Follett, considered that the young soldier was the flower of the flock. And here [George] Gleig – afterwards Chaplain General – then "the Subaltern," made his *coup d'essai* in arms.

At San Sebastian, in a rather indifferent hotel but which was, I believe the best in the town we had some real Sherry – *xeres seco*. It was undeniably good, but not good enough to detain us longer than the next day, when we pushed on to Fontarabia – remembered Roncesvalles and the evil destiny of Orlando[21] – the most renowned of the *preux chevaliers* of the Court of Charlemagne and the hero of Ariosto's immortal song – and of the "blast of that dread horn on Fontarabia echoes borne." And then we reached Irun, the frontier between Spain and France, where I recollect nothing remarkable except that we saw the Isle des Faisans – the place at which the Spanish monarch [Philip IV] bestowed the hand of his young and beautiful daughter Maria Theresa upon the French monarch, Louis XIV. Here it was that Velázquez, one of the very best painters the world has ever possessed, came at the king's bidding to arrange the sumptuous pavilion and the other decorations, which were displayed in honour of the betrothal. In consequence of his excursions, it is said that he here contracted an illness under which he sank soon after his return to Madrid, a price too high for such a ceremony – for would it be wrong to say that the value of one Velázquez would far outweigh the worth of the two kings, and the Infanta in the bargain?

We had a most beautiful trip along the coast, visited Biarritz – no such villa as was afterwards built by Napoleon III and his Empress Eugénie, and which became and still is a most fashionable French watering place. We stayed a short time at the old town of Saint-Jean-de-Luz and visited and made a sketch of the Castle – we were delighted with the coast scenery and the distant range of mountains, one feature of which, called Les Trois Couronnes, must never be forgotten; and then returned to Bayonne. We then engaged a carriage, which took us through a most picturesque country to Pau. We visited the old castle, the birthplace of Henry IV.

> *Ce Roi Vaillant*
> *Ce diable a quatre, qui a le triple talent*
> *De boire, et de battre, et de faire le vert galant.*

We heard or remembered the old stories about his heroic mother, who at her father's bidding sang a country ditty in the midst of her agony, and of his brutal old grandfather, who administered to the *nouveau né* a sip of the strong *vin de Beaune* to qualify him for the hazardous life he was

---

[21] The Italian appellation of Roland, the Carolingian knight who defended Roncesvalles, or Roncevaux, with his life

about to begin, and we gazed with due wonder at the well-preserved turtle shell that served him for a cradle. What we most admired was the great panorama from the terrace, and the snow-clad mountain range in the distance.

Several days were afterwards employed in visiting the principal towns of the Pyrenees. I wish I had time enough and that my memory served me to describe these places. I recollect, however, the interest we took in the famous bathing town, or rather villages in which warm water is so prevalent and abundant as to retain to this day their old reputation for curing, or at least relieving, persons suffering from gout or rheumatism and almost all the other "many ills to which the flesh is heir."[22] We were interested in and mused at the strange mixture of old world and modern fashions in the houses and accommodations, and delighted with the wild and picturesque scenery. We visited Eaux-Bonnes and Eaux-Chaudes, Saint-Sauver, and Cauterets, the scene of the Queen of Navarre's collection of stories written in emulation if not in imitation of [Boccaccio's] *Decameron*. Hardly worthy of the well earned fame of the heroic sister of Francis I, who is deservedly renowned as the virtuous and brave Protestant champion in times when fire and the stake were the fate of those who dared to profess the purer faith – and whose title to renown rests upon her having been the patroness and protector of Clément Margot then upon the authorship (if she was the author?) of the *Heptameron*, which passes under her name. They have famous ponies in this district – hardy, wiry, full of courage and perfectly sure-footed. Of these qualities, we had abundant proof in an excursion we made up the mountain road leading towards Spain. Lofty and precipitous rocks on the left, and on the right the steep descent to the roaring stream many fathoms below. A passage this, not with serious danger for ordinary horses and travelers, but convenient for the *contrabandistas* who, it is reported, carry on a considerable traffic here to the detriment of the Spanish Custom House authorities. Less brave than Hotspur who talks about "o'er walking a current roaring loud on the unsteadfast footing of a spear,"[23] we sped our way safely though, I do mind to confess not without some occasional

---

[22] *Hamlet*, Act III, Scene I.
[23] *Henry IV, Part 1*, Act I, Scene III

anxiety. The sky was clear – the rugged outline of the frontier mountains striking grand – La Brèche de Roland clear and distinct, as if the mighty hero had left the mark of his prowess but recently. We stayed awhile on the road to gaze and wonder at the singular place where large masses of rock had been tossed in such mysterious confusion as to justify the name chaos by which it is called. It cannot be called beautiful nor even interesting, but it has an impressive and weird effect on the beholders. Another of the wonders of this ride was Le Cirque de Gavarnie. It looks like an old and shapeless amphitheater of enormous extent, and obviously the product of some convulsion of nature which passes the ability of any but a profound geologist to explain – and he perhaps knows as little about it as I do.

At all events we had a most agreeable excursion – the views of inexhaustible variety and novelty. The abundant and vigorous growth of the box tree, which clothes the sides of the nearer mountains and down to the edge of the noisy rapid river being one of the most striking features. We passed Tarbes and saw the plain in which Orthez stands (Wood's story of the Duke of Wellington and the hostess)[24] and were reminded of Froissart's mention of the district [in the Hundred Years War] and of the last of the battles [of the Napoleonic Wars], in which the Duke of Wellington expelled the French Army under [Marshal Jean-de-Dieu] Soult from the [Iberian] peninsula.

Agen was our next stopping place. We did not go to look for the great (!) Provençal poet [Jacques Jasmin], whom some of the French critics have the impudence to compare with [Robert] Burns, nor did we repair to the barber's shop in which this child of the Muses plies his more useful art, enlivened occasionally by the doggerel in which he and his admirers delight. A steamboat on the Garonne carried us to Bordeaux. We passed thence to Paris and returned home all the better in mind and body for our holiday.

In the Vacation of 1854, we made rather an extensive trip. The party consisted of ourselves and Sis – and three of the boys. We went, I

---

[24] Numerous legends hold that the Duke of Wellington tempted fate in this region by visiting French taverns, where he drank and gamed with French soldiers, and may have defended himself with a pistol in an ambush by French hussars.

think, by rail to Dijon – and thence to Châlons. At this letter place, we embarked upon what seemed to be a somewhat crazy boat, which was crowded by market people and their merchandise bound for Lyons. The weather was fine and the views full of interest. We passed Trévoux, once a seat of learning and of renown in the literary world, which was superseded by the spreading influence of the all-conquering press, and the famous river-reach of Villefranche. *"L'Anse Villefranche est le plus beau lieu de France,"* is an old local brag, and though its literal truth may be questioned, it is undoubtedly charming scenery. The ancient and beautiful church is one of its most remarkable features. We did not pass some parts of this voyage without a certain anxiety caused principally by the condition of our boat, but augmented by the stupidity of the passengers whose noises and restlessness made us contemplate the possibility of a capsize. We held a council of war and determined that as the river was not very wide and as three of us could swim (Hugh had gone on alone to Lyons) we should be able to carry our two ladies safely to shore and made up our minds to the worst that might befall us. Happily, our excursions were not called into request, and we reached the quay at Lyons, *quittes pour la peur*. If I had more time, I could say more about the beauties of the Saône, and the towns of Châlons and Maçons, and the churches and hospitals and famous burgundy, which deserved all the praise the hardest drinker could bestow upon it.

From Lyons (After a melancholy visit to the cemetery), we went by diligence over the Jura to Geneva, whence we enjoyed, along the most picturesque road, the views of the ever-lovely lake and the glorious majesty of Mont Blanc. I have nothing to say about the city, so we proceeded to Vevey and thence to a newly opened hotel or boarding house called the Byron, situated at the farther end of the lake on the road to Sion. During the fortnight we passed here, we made several most pleasant excursions by land and water. We ascended the mountains, visited the Castle of Chillon and saw the pillared dungeon whence [François] Bonivard "appealed from tyranny to God." We rowed to the shore opposite Vevey and contemplated the scenery, which the too potent pen of Rousseau has made immortal for evil and mischief. Our boys had a narrow escape from a dangerous boating excursion to which they were tempted by a very good-natured, half crazy, Quaker-bred man who was the father (or grandfather?) of Mrs. Hardwick. At the issue of the Rhône into the lake, the sudden meeting and rush of the waters forms a kind of whirlpool and is dangerous always and trying, even to skillful boatmen. Our people were more indebted to their good luck than to their skill or knowledge for getting out of the difficulties they encountered. However, they did escape, with no other mischief than a thorough drenching, and we fortunately knew nothing of their danger until it was over and passed. I need to not say how thankful (and angry) we were when we heard the history at large! We met here my good friend and frequent combatant in Chancery, Richard Malins, who was traveling with his wife and niece (now our pleasant acquaintance, Miss Cary Malins.)

We engaged here in Lombardy Vellurino, who had commodious carriage – big enough for our party, with four little wiry, active horses. Traveling about thirty miles a day, in the cool, he carried us to Berne, Lucerne, and Zurich, showed us the falls of the Rhine at Schaffhausen, and then took us through the Black Forest to Strassbourg. We lingered here a while and were delighted with the grand old Cathedral, wonder-stricken with the marvelous mechanical ingenuity of the Great Clock, which teaches astronomy and geometry and arithmetic and would tell your fortune if you only had the patience to listen, and the skill to understand its mysterious lessons.

We could not wait long enough to profit by all that we might have learned. So we contented ourselves with looking at the statues of Gutenberg and of [Napoleon's] dare-devil General Kléber, and other works of art, ancient and modern, which adorned this famous city.

And then we bold along merrily, chiefly by rail. We stayed awhile at Nancy, where we saw the tombs and statues of former great heroes and potentates, Dukes of Burgundy, and looked reverently upon the faded glories of the Toison d'Or, and the more moderate amenities (as the Scottish call them) with which the dethroned monarch, Stanislaus [Leczyński, King of Poland], decorated this his last residence, the park and gardens and especially the gates are well worthy of notice as elegant specimens of graceful frivolity and the art of adornment of residential establishments. And we did not forget that Nancy was the birthplace and home (when he had a home) of that eccentric genius Jacques Callot, the George Cruikshank of his day, the past master of the etching point.

At Bar-le-Duc, we did not forget to lay in a provision of the famous fruit, preserved in transparent jelly, for which this city is renowned all over the world, but it was so nice that I am not sure that much of it found its way with us across the Channel. We stopped at Rheims, only long enough to visit the grand monumental Cathedral. Our time was rapidly drawing to an end. We resolved not to return home through Paris, and therefore stopped at Meaux, whence on the following day there was a train direct to Boulogne.

We were lodged at one point of the oldest looking hotels I had ever seen in France, and under the old-fashioned sign of La Sirène. It was kept by a very aged hostess, very formal and dress and manner, and very courteous, who promised us a good dinner and who kept her promise. I do not recollect of what the menu consisted but it was really admirable and cooked to perfection. We had no such dinner in all our wanderings. So good was it that in order to keep it in mind and to celebrate it, and perhaps because we had not availed ourselves of the opportunity of drinking champagne at Rheims - its own native country - we ordered a bottle of that delicious vin d'Aÿ, that which one of the older poets called *"ce liqueur charmant, qui console."*

Ce long hiver qu'on appelle la vieillesse and the wine was as good as the dinner. On expressing our satisfaction with the latter, the old lady said it ought to be good for it was the work of one of the best cooks in France – and by way of explanation she told us it was prepared by her son, who assisted her in her business and was the support and solace of her old age. He had been for several years the *chef de cuisine* of the former Empress Joséphine. And upon her death, having made a sufficient provision for his *avenir*, he had declined to take any other employment but devoted himself to cheering his mother's declining years and the cultivation of his garden. We were introduced to the son, who was apparently between fifty and sixty years old, and we found him very civil, modest, and intelligent, with a touch of politeness that he had probably acquired in the course of his imperial employment. On the following morning, he showed us his garden and greenhouse, which were skillfully kept, and gave us a plant of his own raising, he said, *Le Souvenir de Malmaison*.[25] From that plant, which I brought home with great care, I have raised scores of beautiful rose bushes which are still the joy and pride of my garden.

From Meaux we came home without stopping and thus ended our trip of 1854.

Dieppe

I ought to have mentioned much earlier a long vacation we passed at Dieppe. I am afraid that this is not the only defect in the chronology of this irregular history. I regret that I did not keep a more perfect record of our movements, but I have none, nor any notes of my own, and with the exception of such memorandums as dear Sis has scraped together for me, and which I have found most useful in all that I have hitherto written, I am compelled to rely upon my memory such as it is.

We crossed from New Haven, and after a good passage in fine weather – not without some torment from the *mal de mer* under which we all suffered, more or less (accept my dear wife who was a fearless sailor and in those days was never sick nor sorry), and found ourselves in the hotel on the quay. We stayed here two or three days, looked about us and soon found a house which suited us admirably. We did not care for a view of the sea, so we did not bestow much time in examining them. They were mere seaside lodging houses – Dieppe was not then the fashionable bathing place it has since become, although there were a good many visitors, the shore was very shallow, the sands very extensive, and for hours together bare and burning for nearly a mile. Taking a header into the water was impossible, and swimming except at high-water out of the question. The cliffs were lofty and white. Along the coast was striking – and as much as we could see of the inland country promising and inviting. By hint of inquiring and hunting, we at length found a strange looking house in a quarter mostly on foot, but sometimes ponies and donkeys lent us their help. We visited an old worn-out building, all that remains of the almost princely establishment of a certain Augo, a famous *arenateur* (i.e.

---

[25] The specially bred rose had been created in 1843 and named for Malmaison, Joséphine's final home, which had marvelous rose gardens.

a shipowner, merchant and occasionally pirate), who established a valuable commerce with places on the African Coast and especially introduced to Dieppe a trade in ivory, which remained for several centuries a source of great profit and of which some faint traces are supposed to remain in the Ivory carving which is still to some extent cultivated in Dieppe. Augo is said to have been patronized by Louis XI, and was greatly encouraged by Francis I, to whom he gave a royal entertainment in his Château of Varengavelle, by which name La Maison d'Augo it is still called. The poor man seems to have outlived his good fortune and to have died in misery and disgrace – "deserted at his utmost need by those his former bounty fed." (Dryden, *Alexander's Feast, or the Power of Music*)

Le Château d'Arques remains a memorial of one of the most important victories of Henry IV, and a very remarkable monument it is. Its massive walls and its commanding position seeming to defy the inroads of time and the change of fortune.

We also passed an idle, pleasant afternoon at the oyster beds at Neufville and Le Phare aux Huîtres, where several acres of shallow saltwater are devoted to the production and cultivation of the mollusks, which are served to the visitors with bread and butter, and a thin white wine.

Upon the whole, we passed a very pleasant time at Dieppe, and the more agreeably because we were all together.

I made several other journeys of which I have a less distinct recollection. One was to Turin, a most interesting city, with the white summits of the Alps shining over the crowded streets, and a magnificent opera house and the bright palace, with the Basilica of Superga crowning a mountain in the distance.

To Milan, where I saw all that remained of the marvelous *Cenacolo* (*Last Supper*) of Leonardo, and thought over the story (lately verified) of his having avenged himself on the troublesome intendant who complained to the Pope that instead of Leonardo working upon the wall, he spent hours in listlessly gazing upon the work, by introducing the rascal's ill favoured face as that of Judas Iscariot in the picture. The truth was that the painter was endeavoring by long and deep contemplation to collect as well as he could the form and expression of the divine lineaments of the Saviour. Little indeed of that now remains. An attempt was made by Dr. Boxall to rescue that admirable head from the rain which is pervading the whole of the fresco. Boxall has done all that could be done, and Lord Coleridge is now the owner of Boxall's cartoon.

I heard a gaunt, bare-footed friar preach from the balcony surrounding one of the massive columns at the entrance to the nave of the Cathedral on the feast day of the Virgin Mary – and I shall never forget the impression he produced upon a multitudinous audience as he described to them in great detail the agonies which the Mother must have endured at witnessing the sufferings of her divine son during his passion. Groans, cried, shrieks. Frantic transports of grief followed and often interrupted the preacher, who, as it seemed, "wielded at will fierce democracy" (they were mostly people of the lower orders) and captivated and transported their souls.

At Easter 1837, I had made a journey to the cemetery at Lyons. I had announced my intention some time before. Reason (I forget what) had doomed me to travel alone, always a most unsatisfactory operation, when, by good fortune, Charles Roupess offered himself as my traveling companion! He only wanted to fill up his holiday and did not care when or where he went. I most gladly accepted his offer. We met at Folkestone at the time fixed and thence to Paris by the accustomed route. Years – many years – have since gone by, and the travelers are much changed. Charley was always cheerful – never in buoyant spirits, but good-tempered and willing to take things as they came – and full of a quiet, dry humour which could extract fun out of the most unpromising materials. Now alas! He suffers under a complication of nervous maladies of which rheumatism is not the only one, nor the worst. He comes to see me sometimes and we try to make the best we can of the bad times that have overtaken us by conjuring up the ghosts of past gaieties – not without regret that they can never come again. We passed several days in Paris, which was then more amusing than I have found it to be upon recent visits. The aspect of the city was then infinitely more picturesque than it afterwards became under the improving (?) hand of the Baron Haussmann. All the old buildings have disappeared. The grim forms have given place to the vitruvian lines and curves of modern taste and the rich time – colourful tints are effaced and have fled under the white-washing of the plaster of Paris. Worse even than this, the demolitions of these socialistic friends have erased the Tuileries and many other edifices, public and private, which were rich in the memories of former days.

However, we made the best we could of it. We dined at Philippe's and at the Trois frères Provençaux, and at the more humble but not less satisfactory Boeuf à la Mode. We saw the everlasting Palais Royal and at least half a dozen other playhouses, and drank beer on the boulevards and limonade at the *cafés chantants*.

We were grandly lodged at the Hôtel du Louvre. They offered us first two frowsy, ill-lighted garrets at the top of the lofty building, and upon our expressing our disgust at such quarters the majordomo suggested that as we were two single men he would put us up separate beds in a large salon on the first floor, which with the help of large folding screens would be as good as separate chambers. We did not like the thought of going farther and perhaps faring worse, so we submitted and, upon the whole, we did pretty well, though it was at first rather oppressing to occupy so magnificent a lodging. I dare say I snored, but Roupell's corner was so far from mine that he could not have heard me.

The railway to Lyons was not at that time completed, so we were obliged to stop at Dijon – and, as that took up several hours, it was expedient to provide for our recess cities on the road. The buffets were not, as we were told, to be relied on, so like experienced travelers, as we both were, we bought in the Marché de Saint-Honoré a magnificent fowl – *une belle volaille*, is its French appellation, and carried it to a *rotisseur* who promised to have it beautifully cooked by the next morning. The artist kept his word most satisfactorily and made good Boileau's praise of him *"On se fait cuisiner – on est né rotisseur."*

It was really a stroke of genius. With two rolls and some slices of ham from the *chartier* - and a bottle of Médoc – we filled a basket and regaled sumptuously throughout the tedious and uninteresting journey to Dijon when we generously abandoned our basket and its greatly diminished contents to the railway guard.

We stayed at Dijon two days, saw the museum with the admirable sculptures on the tomb of the Duke of Burgundy and the churches, and were reminded of the only joke Bethell is said to have made and which he stole ready-made from Piron.

Thence to Lyons, where the sad object of my journey being accomplished, we prepared to return. I bought two silk dresses (Lyons supposed to be famous for that manufacturer), one for my dear wife and the other for Sis. Back to Paris, then home.

I asked Roupell the other day to help me with his recollections of this trip. He looked up his diary with great difficulty, but there was not a scrap nor a hint of any sort to gathered from it.

The Polygon Building, where Sir James Bacon spent his childhood

The old Sadler's Wells Theatre, attended by Sir James in his youth

Sir James Bacon pictured during his middle years

Sir James Bacon in old age

Sir James Bacon as Vice Chancellor and member of the Privy Council,
published in the *Illustrated London News*, 12 November, 1870.

Compton Beach House, country home of Sir James Bacon

Cartoon of Sir James Bacon, celebrated for his witty judgments

Cartoon of Sir James Bacon published in the weekly satirical magazine Vanity
Fair c. 1886

Sir James Bacon in old age seated with his daughter, Lydia Lawrence, and surrounded by members of his family. On his right is her daughter, Susan Lawrence, later one of the first women members of Parliament, and Laura Lawrence. Below are her other two daughters, Frances Norton with her son, Mark, and Helen Gordon Clark with her son, Michael.

Standing is his son-in-law Nathaniel Tertius Lawrence and his grandson, James Lawrence.

THE LIBRARY
HOUSE OF LORDS
LONDON SW1A 0PW

Enquiries/ 020 7219 3242
or 020 7219 5433
Fax: 020 7219 6396
Direct Line: 020 7219

26th June, 2000

Dear Mr. de Marcellus,

It was most kind of you to allow us to take a copy of "Recollections of the Vice Chancellor Sir James Bacon, P.C. written for his children". This is a fascinating account, with much interesting comment on the legal dignitaries of the time. I am very pleased to have obtained a copy for the Library and we are most grateful to you for the trouble you took in bringing this volume over the Atlantic.

Sincerely,

David L. Jones

D. L. Jones
Librarian

Ms Juliette de Marcellus,
357 Crescent Drive,
Palm Beach,
Florida 33480,
U.S.A.

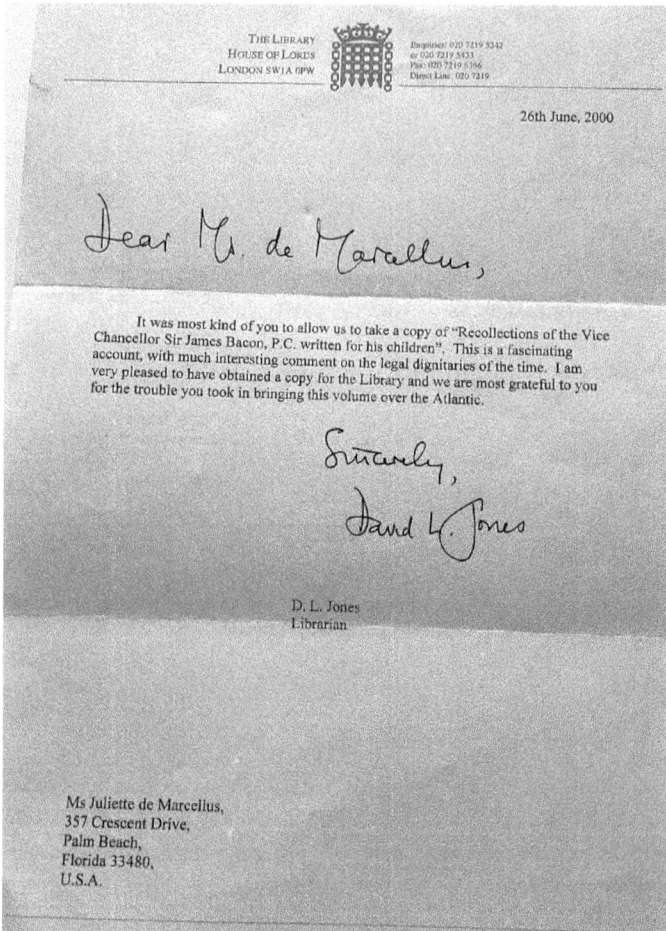

Letter of thanks from the House of Lords Librarian

www.ingramcontent.com/pod-product-compliance
Lightning Source LLC
Chambersburg PA
CBHW060416100426
42812CB00037B/3485/J